THE
SPIRITUAL
SCIENCE
OF EMMA CURTIS HOPKINS

THE
SPIRITUAL
SCIENCE
OF EMMA CURTIS HOPKINS

12 LESSONS TO A NEW TRANSCENDENT YOU

edited by RUTH L. MILLER

LIBRARY OF
HIDDEN KNOWLEDGE

ATRIA BOOKS
New York London Toronto Sydney New Delhi

Hillsboro, Oregon

ATRIA BOOKS
A Division of Simon & Schuster, Inc.
1230 Avenue of the Americas
New York, NY 10020

BEYOND WORDS
20827 N.W. Cornell Road, Suite 500
Hillsboro, Oregon 97124–9808
503-531-8700 / 503-531-8773 fax
www.beyondword.com

Copyright © 2013 by Ruth L. Miller

Original text for *Esoteric Philosophy: Deeper Teachings in Spiritual Science*, published by High Watch Fellowship, 1925.

Managing editor: Lindsay S. Brown
Editor: Gretchen Stelter
Copyeditor: Jade Chan
Proofreader: Linda M. Meyer
Design: Devon Smith
Composition: William H. Brunson Typography Services

First Atria Books/Beyond Words hardcover edition October 2013

For more information about special discounts for bulk purchases, please contact Simon & Schuster Special Sales at 1-866-506-1949 or business@simonandschuster.com.

The Simon & Schuster Speakers Bureau can bring authors to your live event. For more information or to book an event, contact the Simon & Schuster Speakers Bureau at 1-866-248-3049 or visit our website at www.simonspeakers.com.

Manufactured in the United States of America

10 9 8 7 6 5 4 3 2 1

Library of Congress Cataloging-in-Publication Data

The spiritual science of Emma Curtis Hopkins : 12 lessons to a new transcendent you / edited by Ruth L. Miller. — First Atria Books/Beyond Words hardcover edition.
       pages   cm. — (Library of hidden knowledge)
    1. Hopkins, Emma Curtis. 2. Spiritual life. 3. Occultism. 4. New Thought.
 I. Miller, Ruth L., 1948- editor of compilation.
 BF1999.S64   2013
 289.9′8092—dc23

                                                                    2013013889

ISBN 978-1-58270-420-3
ISBN 978-1-4767-2864-3 (ebook)

The corporate mission of Beyond Words Publishing, Inc.: *Inspire to Integrity*

CONTENTS

ORIGINAL TEXT
ESOTERIC PHILOSOPHY: DEEPER TEACHINGS IN SPIRITUAL SCIENCE
AS PUBLISHED IN 1925

Note from the Editor

This book is the seventh in the Library of Hidden Knowledge, a series of books originally written by philosopher-teachers who were famous in the late-nineteenth or early-twentieth century. We've chosen specific texts by each of these authors and "translated" them into guides for living a healthy, prosperous life in the twenty-first century, providing summary points, modern examples and scientific explanations, and exercises to support their text. Then we've followed our translation with the author's original text. Our hope is that having read through the modernized language and format, the reader will better comprehend the complex prose and antiquated references that were normal for the authors and readers of that time.

Like the other authors in this series, Emma Curtis Hopkins was famous for both her lectures and her writing during her lifetime and beyond. Also like the others, she spoke and wrote in flowery prose and referred to many ancient and contemporary sources that she assumed her listeners were familiar with. She also used the only form of the Christian Bible available to her, the King James Version, and often followed its complex sentence structure.

To make her ideas more accessible to modern readers, we've generally simplified her text by shortening sentences and adding headings and subheadings, using the New International Version for biblical quotes (with occasional use of other versions if the language was clearer). We've also expanded her use of other religions' scriptures and updated the examples she used to illustrate her points.

Most of the books in this series were originally lectures that were later turned into essays and published by their authors, and this is no exception. The material in *Esoteric Philosophy: Deeper Teachings in Spiritual Science* is what Hopkins taught her advanced students and turned into a book late in her life so that they would have a guide when she was no longer teaching. This book was designed to help people who had explored the basic teachings from her earlier works and classes, such as those found in Florence Scovel Shinn's *The Game of Life and How to Play It*,[1] and were ready to take their understanding and practice to a new level.

Hopkins may well have been the most influential teacher of what nineteenth-century psychologist William James called "the religion of positive thought," which is now known as the New Thought movement. Her twelve-step process was the basis for the organizations that became known as Unity, Divine Science, and Religious Science (Centers for Spiritual Living).

Because it is such a powerful tool for getting beyond our society's limited ideas about who we are and what we're capable of doing, thousands of people who've used it have seen a change in their experience. And people who do her practice faithfully for several weeks have generally found that their health, relationships, and finances shift to healthier states.[2] Those who not only do the process for themselves but share it with others have become powerful healers and teachers in their own right, as the existence of so many branches of the New Thought movement testifies.

In part, this is because Hopkins was a teacher of science and mathematics first and a metaphysician only after the observed evidence proved its effectiveness. Her logical process provided a bridge between the scientific method applied to observable phenomena and the purely intuitive experience she came to call "high mysticism." As a result, students from all walks of life, from engineer to minister, from housekeeper to college professor, were able to follow her teaching and experience powerful results.

Still, Hopkins's writings were often difficult to comprehend. She offered a view of the world and our place in it that was based in ideals and absolutes, and she used language in a unique way. What others called God she might call the Absolute or the Eternal or the Infinite Abiding or any of forty or more terms. What others thought of as most important, such as one's circumstances, she saw as only indicative of past thought patterns that could be easily negated. What others assumed to be limited she would describe in the broadest of terms, saying, for example, "mind" instead of "the mind" to help the student step outside habits of limitation.

Her unique way of thinking and speaking helps the reader expand beyond normal thought processes, and we've attempted to maintain her style, though where it leads only to more confusion, we've replaced it with a more familiar form. Throughout this book, we've made every effort to give you the essence of her remarkable approach to life and human potential.

We hope you find these teachings as valuable as so many thousands have before.

GETTING THE MOST FROM THIS BOOK

As with all the books in the Library of Hidden Knowledge, we recommend reading the first half of the book—the modern translation—and then scanning the second half—the original text—to find the parts that leap off the page. The ideal next step is to do the exercises in the first half, using the author's original text as additional support in the process. Then, reading the original (and Hopkins's other works) carefully will be much more meaningful.

With Hopkins's lessons, though, there's another level to be aware of. The first six lessons apply to our personal lives and development; they are how she would have us start our day. Ideally, we would read and practice lesson 1 on Monday mornings, lesson 2 on Tuesday mornings, and so forth, through Saturday.[3]

The last six lessons apply to the people and world around us. These lessons are what Hopkins would have us focus on in the afternoon, generally taking time around noon to consider one lesson each day. Ideally, then, we'd look at lesson 7 Monday afternoons, lesson 8 Tuesdays, and so forth.[4]

After you've gone through the book as a whole, you may find, as so many have already, that using her lessons in this way is a powerful method for advancing your spiritual life.

INTRODUCTION

E mma Curtis Hopkins is called the "teacher of teachers" in the New Thought movement because, literally, every founder of every tradition in the movement studied with her or one of her students. Charles and Myrtle Fillmore, founders of what is now called Unity Worldwide, were among her first students. Ernest Holmes, founder of the Institute of Religious Science and the Centers for Spiritual Living, was her last. In between were the Brooks sisters and Malinda Cramer, founders of Divine Science, the Rix sisters, founders of the Home of Truth Spiritual Center, and hundreds of others.

Hopkins was an extraordinary teacher whom all her students loved. The eldest daughter of a Connecticut farmer who lost his arm in the Civil War, she was one of the young women who took over the teaching positions that had been vacated by the young men who went to fight in that war. She taught mathematics, science, and literature in girls' schools and high schools until she married an equally brilliant teacher named George Hopkins and bore their son, John. Then, being a married woman in that time and place, she was no longer considered fit to teach in a school, so she taught her younger sister and son until he reached his teens and went to the Merchant Marine Academy around 1890.[1]

Hopkins was also a scholar. She loved mathematics and ancient literature, having read Pythagoras in the original Greek, and studied the writings of the early Christian mystics in the original Latin. From references in her texts, it also appears she was able to read German and understood the difference between the Aramaic spoken at the time of the Roman Empire and the Hebrew used in the Jewish temple and Torah. As her interest in religion and mysticism grew, she also read the Tao Te Ching, the Zend-Avesta, the Egyptian Book of the Dead, the Qur'an, the Bhagavad Gita, the Upanishads, and as many of the Buddha's sutras as she could find.

Hopkins became interested in alternative healing practices when traditional medicine failed to help her family. She and her family were living in New Hampshire when a neighbor invited her for tea to meet a visiting friend. The friend was Mrs. Mary Baker Eddy, and the tea turned out to be an introductory lecture on Eddy's Christian Science.

Hopkins was not impressed. She knew enough of the biology and chemistry of the day to consider what Eddy said to be a matter of superstition rather than fact, and so she dismissed the event from her mind.

A few months later, however, the Hopkins family suffered from a respiratory ailment, which was not uncommon in a time of dirt roads, open fires, horse-drawn transportation, and no vacuum cleaners. Doctors could not help, and things were approaching a crisis when the neighbor begged to be allowed to do one of Eddy's treatments for the family. Seeing no harm and no real alternative, Hopkins allowed it and was amazed to see her son, sister, and husband fully recovered shortly thereafter. She decided she must know more and immediately wrote to Eddy, requesting that she have the opportunity to learn from the teacher herself.

Eddy agreed, and Hopkins was enrolled in the Basic Class at the Massachusetts Metaphysical College in Boston, graduating in December 1883. Hopkins posted a small ad, offering Christian Science treatments in Boston, which was displayed in the February 1884 issue of the *Christian Science Journal*. She had arranged to stay at the college in Boston a few days a week to offer treatments and assist with the production of the journal, returning home to New Hampshire in between.

She was soon listed as editor of the journal, writing articles and responding to letters through September 1885. Then in October she was informed that there was no longer a place for her to stay at the college, and her services as editor were no longer required. No explanation was given, but it appears that her article in the September issue comparing Eddy favorably to other mystical writers was contrary to the new organizational policy: there was only one metaphysician to be recognized, and that was Eddy herself.

Stunned, Hopkins went home to New Hampshire, and though she requested an explanation and never got one, she never spoke against the woman she called her "beloved teacher" in all the years that followed. Her only comment on the matter, some years later, was, "They did not seem to understand my complicated way of explaining myself."[2]

Instead, in the face of this sudden reversal Hopkins applied the fundamental principles she'd been writing about and continued to affirm that "God, the omnipotent omnipresence, is good; therefore, I am surrounded by good and only good."

She was soon offered a position in Chicago as interim editor of J. A. Swartz's *Mental Science Magazine and Mind-Cure Journal*. The magazine presented articles and letters by people exploring the ideas of Eddy and others who used the mental healing process that Phineas Parkhurst Quimby had developed in the 1850s.

So in December 1885, Hopkins, along with her younger sister, husband, and son, packed their belongings, got on a train, and moved from their small home in New Hampshire to the bustling city of Chicago. There they rented a much larger home, and Hopkins placed an ad in the local paper, offering mental healing treatments and, for select guests, a place to stay while undergoing treatment.

Mary Plunkett, another student of Eddy's, joined them, and she and Hopkins formed the Emma Curtis Hopkins College of Christian Science. Basic Classes were offered at the (then astounding) fee of $50 for the series of twelve lessons. Students were expected to practice daily between classes and fill their minds with the ideas being presented in order to shift their mental framework and develop the healing power.

The combination of her reputation from her work on Eddy's journal, her exposure in her new editorial position, and the newspaper ads worked. The Hopkins family was quite comfortable for the next couple of years. They even bought a large home for themselves and their occasional student-guests. Hopkins's students were encouraged to internalize the material she taught, heal themselves, and then go out to teach and heal others, interpreting the material in their own way as they did so. As a result, dozens of branches of the Hopkins Metaphysical Association were formed around the country, where her students took her materials and offered them to their friends and neighbors.

Then in May 1888, everything fell apart again. Her partner Mary Plunkett returned to the East Coast, taking their administrative records with her to begin a program in New York, and Hopkins's husband George took their son back to New England. Hopkins knew that, somehow, it was all for the best, even if she didn't see it clearly at first.

It was one of her graduates who helped her see what was to be done next. A Methodist minister helped her form a new organization, licensed by the State of Illinois, with a board of directors and expanded faculty. She raised the funds to do so by printing her lecture notes for the Basic Class and selling them. They're in print today as *Class Lessons of 1888*.[3]

Those first lessons were very similar to what Eddy had taught Hopkins, but as she continued to teach and study, Hopkins's ideas expanded and moved in some different directions. She began to include more of the writings of early Christian mystics, as well as those of the Asian religious traditions. She also integrated more of the thoughts and words of Ralph Waldo Emerson, Thomas Carlyle, and Emanuel Swedenborg.

Eddy was not pleased and wrote in her *Christian Science Journal* that Hopkins was dangerous, was teaching lessons with errors, and didn't have either the proper training or the right to teach at all. Still, Hopkins spoke highly of her teacher as she went forward on her own journey to discover and teach the highest Truth she could.

By 1889 Hopkins had found her stride. The seminary did well as people completed the Basic Class and then went on to the Advanced Class and, for some, additional coursework in Bible studies, world religions, and studies of other mystical writers. Soon graduates were being asked by their own students to function as ministers, rather than simply as teachers, by offering Sunday services. In response to the need, the coursework was expanded and the ministers on the board began ordaining graduates.

Hopkins taught regularly, but more and more, other faculty members taught the classes and students did the healing work. She traveled a bit, speaking in San Francisco, London, and New York to classes of 250 or more students and establishing more branches of the Hopkins Association. She visited her husband and son in New England several times and traveled to Veracruz, Mexico, in 1896, when her son was ill there during one of his many voyages as a mariner.

Meanwhile, her husband returned to Chicago for visits, but in 1901 he divorced her, citing abandonment, and then remarried a few years later. Hopkins realized that this was one of the ways that, as she described it in her tenth lesson, the "world comes unglued" as people move along their spiritual path, and she released him with love as she went forward on her own path.

In 1893, when the World's Fair came to Chicago, Hopkins made a radical decision. Rather than competing with Eddy's Christian Science in the World's Parliament of Religions Pavilion, she presented the Hopkins Association, whose branches now numbered in the hundreds, in the Women's Pavilion. Their booth presented Hopkins's approach to healing as a way for women to care for themselves and their families and to have an income stream of their own, which was still a radical idea in that day and age.

By June of that year, according to college records, 110 students had graduated and been ordained through her seminary, and more than eleven thousand people had experienced the elimination of physical and emotional distress through her treatments. That was the year that Charles and Myrtle Fillmore, founders of Unity in Kansas City, Missouri, completed the Advanced Course and launched the teaching aspect of their organization. Annie Rix Militz, who with her sister later cofounded Home of Truth (sometimes called Sanctuaries of Truth), was on the staff of the seminary that year and later became a board member.

Over the next few years, Hopkins and her students published a number of small books based on her lecture notes and the series of Bible study articles she'd written for the Chicago newspaper *Inter Ocean*. Most of these have been reprinted in recent years by Rev. P. Joanna Rodgers, a leading scholar on all things relating to Hopkins, and by WiseWoman Press in Vancouver, Washington, and are available online. A list of Hopkins's titles appears at the end of this book.

Hopkins's study of mystical writings took her into a deeper and deeper quiet. She became a true mystic and began to realize that focusing on communion with the divine was becoming her primary calling. In her final book, *High Mysticism*, she wrote that the mystical life calls us to own less and less and become less and less engaged in the world around us. Yet she continued to teach some and to serve as an administrator at the seminary, always affirming that the highest good was surrounding and sustaining her.

Then in 1905, a Hopkins Association in New Orleans requested permission to create a seminary there. She agreed and helped them get started that fall. Apparently, she saw the new organization as fulfilling her obligation because, after classes were complete in June 1906, Hopkins closed the doors of the Chicago seminary, packed up a suitcase with her belongings, and walked away.

For almost two decades thereafter, Hopkins was a traveling teacher. She would spend the summers on the farm she grew up on, now managed by the younger sister who had lived with her so many years ago. Then she'd go to New York in the fall and winter and perhaps Philadelphia, Boston, or even Europe in the spring. One year she spent the spring in Taos, New Mexico, with New York socialite Mabel Dodge Luhan, who was a friend of artist Georgia O'Keefe and writer D. H. Lawrence. Luhan also arranged for a number of the artists and writers who attended her New York salons to work with Hopkins, often paying for their treatments.[4]

Among Hopkins's students during that time were New Yorkers Dr. Harriet Emilie Cady and Florence Scovel Shinn, both of whom went on to teach and write foundation texts for the New Thought movement: Cady's *Lessons in Truth* is fundamental for Unity students, and Shinn's *The Game of Life and How to Play It* is widely popular and considered essential reading for Adult Children of Alcoholics. (It is the fourth book in the Library of Hidden Knowledge series.)

Those familiar with the twelve-step process used in Alcoholics Anonymous and related addiction programs may wonder if there's a link to Hopkins's lessons—and in fact, there is. Bill W., cofounder of AA, worked closely with a young man whose mother was secretary to Rev. Emmet Fox in New York City through the 1930s. Fox had studied with the Fillmores and was ordained by Nona Brooks of Divine Science, both of whom Hopkins had trained. Fox's Wednesday evening services, which filled Madison Square Garden, were often the after-meeting gathering place for that first group of AA members, and his book *Sermon on the Mount* is often called the "second Big Book."

In 1918 the newly formed International New Thought Alliance elected Hopkins to the position of president. She attended the conference and presented the first version of *High Mysticism*, her final integration of the teachings and possibilities available to every individual willing to do the practice. While there, she met with many of her now-famous former students and encountered one young man named Ernest Holmes, who was interviewing every healer he could meet with. For no known reason, she refused his request for an interview.

In 1923, while visiting New York, Hopkins experienced a sudden heart ailment, which she described in a letter to Mabel Dodge Luhan as "not so much an illness as God calling an end to a career."[5] She spent most of that year and the next with her sister on the family farm near Killingly, Connecticut.

By the fall of 1924, however, Hopkins felt much better and returned to New York. Again, Holmes, in town on a lecture tour, requested an interview. This time she agreed, and he visited her at her hotel. It turned out, however, that this was not simply an interview, but rather a pressentation of lesson one in her teachings. Holmes agreed to return and completed the series with her, after which he sat down and wrote the first edition of what became the bestselling *The Science of Mind*, which he self-published in 1925.

Hopkins returned to the family farm in Connecticut soon after meeting with Holmes and passed on from her body in the spring of 1925. Members of her association, now called the High Watch Fellowship, were nearby and, as the story goes, one of them was reading some of Hopkins's favorite Bible passages to her as she took her last breaths.

After her death, members of the High Watch Fellowship continued to circulate copies of transcripts of Hopkins's class lectures, and some continued to publish them under various titles well into the 1980s. They did so, usually without copyright or royalties, out of their love for both the material and the teacher. "Beloved Emma," as her more recent students are apt to call her, had inspired thousands to live in a wonderful new way that is based on a totally different understanding of their own nature, as well as that of the world and of divinity. Her followers felt it was important for the work to be made continually available.

From the very first lesson, in all her books and teachings, Hopkins encouraged students to see the logic of the idea that there can be no power except good anywhere, including in ourselves. This idea alone, if allowed to fill one's thoughts and feelings, can transform one's experience of the world—and *has*, for thousands of her students and readers. It sets a mental framework that perceives good more readily and clearly in all circumstances. Beyond that, with every passing day it creates in the practitioner a resonant field that attracts and encourages more of what that person feels is good.

Hopkins's subsequent lessons build on that fundamental basis. She encourages us to release and be done with any ideas that contradict it, so they won't counteract the resonant effect or cause us to misperceive a situation. She gives us tools to help us transcend all conditions and to help others experience the same kind of results. And, by the end of the twelfth lesson, we realize that, truly, we "belong to the soul of the Beloved . . . have put duality away . . . have seen that the two worlds are one."

TITLES

Class Lessons, 1888 (1888)
Scientific Christian Mental Practices (1888)
Judgment Series (1889)
Drops of Gold (1891)
Bible Interpretation Series (1891)
Resumé (1892)
Genesis Series (1894)
High Mysticism (1918)
The Gospel Series in Spiritual Science (collection published in 2006)
Self Treatments including The Radiant I Am (collection published in 2007)

Many of Hopkins's works were published informally or serially during her lifetime and have since become difficult to find. Publishers such as WiseWoman Press and DeVorss & Company have collected many of her works and made them readily available once again.

INTERPRETATION

Modernized for the
Twenty-First-Century Reader

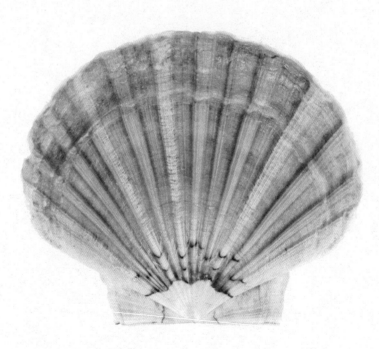

Repentance is turning from expecting some external being to come down and do for us. Repentance is turning to the "I AM," the God, the Lord, the Father at our own center, and reasoning from its presence in us in its glory to its glory in all the earth. "Because I am, thou art." Repentance is turning from judging your life and character by the human and lying aside. It is judging it by the divine and eternal side.

LESSON 1
STATING THE TRUTH

There is a Spiritual Science. It's based on the understanding that mind affects matter whenever words are spoken aloud or in the mind.

It's the science that was taught in the ancient mystery schools—the esoteric teaching offered only to those who had made a commitment to the years required to master it. Spiritual Science is the heart of the mystical—sometimes called metaphysical—religious traditions of today. These religions include those of the New Thought movement—Unity, Science, Religious, Divine Science—as well as Christian Science and most of the indigenous traditions around the world.

It's also the science of quantum mechanics applied to thought and action, as suggested by physicist David Bohm in his lectures and book on "wholeness and the implicate order."[1]

It's the science of the ideal and the real. It's the way that the ideal form, which the ancient Greek philosopher Plato described as existing in the unseen around us,[2] becomes our experience.

This science goes infinitely further than the sciences based on what can be observed with the senses. That means it's not just physical but *metaphysical*. The term *meta* means *beyond*, and what is beyond has no limit. In metaphysics, therefore, far more is implied beyond what is said. There are always meanings within meanings, metaphors within metaphors, inviting the mind to penetrate ever deeper to the infinite core—the wormhole[3] at the center that breaks through to the infinite.

This ability of the mind to penetrate beyond the surface appearance is its freeing sense. How indifferent to appearances the mind becomes when it lets itself loose from the limitations of matter! This esoteric sense is not affected by the outer, or exoteric, circumstances of our normal senses because it penetrates beyond them.

Without exercising this penetrating ability, the mind imprisons itself in matter and so sleeps. But the mind is not content with matter. The mind is not material but something more, and so it seeks to experience more.

Bodies wear out and enter graves when the mind has limited itself to what can be experienced through the five senses. When our thoughts have not penetrated the body as well as the things and objects appearing around it, sensing things not seen, cells and organs are not really nourished and so age and decay.

But when the mind flies beyond words, when it dives below words, when it soars independent of words, it transforms the body. The mind freed from the limitations of perception carries the body's molecules into the light of their true substance. The subatomic connections within them are reinforced from the intelligence woven into the quantum field so that they manifest as a new kind of life, freed from the limitations of time and space.

This is the teaching of mystics and metaphysicians of all ages. It's the ultimate goal of all the sciences.

THE LESSON

The first lesson in the various esoteric traditions is that there is One and One only, and we are part of that One and empowered by our place in it.

In the ancient mystery schools, a student first mastered the basics, the structure and use of language and mathematics and the art of observation and measurement. Then the "as above, so below" relationship of our lives in relation to the circuits of the stars and planets was observed and explained. These were the exoteric teachings offered to all.

Once the student had mastered those, then the inner teachings, including the esoteric doctrine of One Being, would be introduced. Through the millennia, this method exposed the seeker to new possibilities and opened the door to freedom. From Athens to Chartres, from the Nile to Persia to Alhambra, the mysteries were taught and explored through this method.

This esoteric doctrine is expressed in the Judeo-Christian Psalms as "The Lord said unto my lord, sit at My right hand till I make your enemies your footstool."[4] In this text, the Hebrew Lord that speaks to my lord is the one unnameable Infinite Source, called by many names in other traditions: the Highest Brahman, Indescribable God, Great Spirit, Oversoul, Goddess, the First and Uncompanioned One. "My lord" in all of them is the small self, ego, intellect in each of us.

In the text, our ego-self is invited to "sit by My right hand." To "sit at the right hand of" means to speak the words of and do the work of someone in authority. It's a term used in ancient times to describe the administrator or executive officer of the realm, the one who focuses attention on the leader, hears what is to be, speaks the word to others, and makes it so.

The words that my tongue must speak describe where my mind is looking and the work it is doing. Our language always shows what we've been focusing our attention on. And there, where I focus on the Lord, the Source of all being by whatever name, is only Good—Good that is omnipresent (everywhere, in all things), omnipotent (all the power that is), and omniscient (all-pervading intelligence).

My ego-intellect hears in its own fashion. It translates what it hears into common language. It puts into words that I can share what it hears from the Lord, the Highest Brahman, the Oversoul, Spirit. As my own lord, it tells my tongue to speak only of what the Lord has shown me, till misery, ignorance, death, and material limitations all pass away before me.

The Good then reigns. This omnipresent, omnipotent Good is what humanity calls God—by whatever name, be it Allah, Beloved,

Brahman, Christ, the Lord, Krishna, the Mother, the One, or Spirit. All of them are names of the Good.

The Good is Life; Life reigns where we focus our minds on the Good. The Good is Truth; Truth reigns where we focus our minds on the Good. The Good is Love; Love reigns where we focus our minds on the Good, and it shall be the only judge in all things, in all discussions that we let the Good reign over.

If anyone tells us that evil reigns, our tongues tell the irresistible Truth: that the Good is everywhere evil seems to be and the Good shall reign forever. All appearances of wrong, distress, or discord fail when our reasoning minds speak the word that, because the Good is the omnipotence that we call God, it cannot be overthrown.

This is not the exoteric teaching of our culture or even of most religions, but it is Truth. This is not what children are taught when they're being trained in morals and ethics. It is, however, the first esoteric teaching, what mystics come to understand as they leave behind the concrete things of their childhood and begin to deal with the abstract realizations of maturity.

THE OMNIPOTENT GOOD

The Truth concerning the Good is the only Truth. Whoever understands the idea that Truth is the Good tells that Truth, and it will defeat every lie, even every appearance of wrongdoing. If, for example, I took the purse of one who understands this principle, that person wouldn't see theft; they'd see only the fixed Good in me and in the moment. Like the priest in *Les Misérables* who does not condemn the hero of the story, Jean Valjean, when Valjean takes the silver from the table, they'd see the good man for whom something wonderful is taking place. They will rest assured that what is happening in each moment must be the good for all.

This means that anyone who accuses another of wrong thoughts or wrong actions is not speaking Truth. They may be describing accurate appearances but not Truth. The only Truth they could speak concerning anyone describes the fixed Good that is in everyone, every-where. Only then will they experience the omnipotent omnipresence of that Good.

Thus the Highest Lord tells us to see the fixed Good in those we've thought of as our enemies, and they will have no power to hurt us. I once sat in the park near the Haymarket in Chicago as the laborers were gathering, intent to express anger and do harm. I closed my eyes and held to the Truth of their Goodness and their ever-present support and supply, and they disbursed, not knowing why they'd gathered.[5]

So the Highest Lord tells us to see the fixed Good in the action of thieves or terrorists, and that as we do so, the fixed Good will reveal itself even to them. They can't help changing from thieving or terrorizing to kindness when we see the fixed Good in them.

Even children have the ability to see and name the Good; they've not yet forgotten that they're born with it. There's a lovely story of a young boy who asked to spend some time alone with his baby brother. After some discussion the parents agreed, but, concerned that there may be a sibling rivalry problem, left the baby monitor on, just in case. To their great surprise, their four-year-old son leaned over the bars of their brand-new baby's crib and whispered, "Tell me what it's like on the other side. I've almost forgotten." He knew that his own memory of what is Real was fading in the onslaught of his parents' fears and the appearances that make up daily life. He knew how important it is to remember the Good that is the Truth, even though in this culture, this world, we teach our children not to.

Children are taught to hate or fear. They believe in the beauty and kindness of the snake, the spider, and the crocodile till they're told these creatures are neither beautiful nor kind. The color of someone's skin or the slant of another person's eyes is not an issue for them until they're told it must be, just as Oscar Hammerstein tells us in his powerful song "You've Got to Be Carefully Taught" from the musical *South Pacific*.

Everyone who remembers the idea that beauty and kindness are inherent in all things and all people restores themselves to the glory they had before the world as we know it appeared to them. This remembering is what every hermit and saint has aimed for. Those who achieve it have no need to do anything else to eliminate evil, pain, disease, and death from their lives or world. They have only to "sit on the right hand of the Lord," to see and speak only of the Good in all things, all people, all principle, and, as the psalm quoted earlier tells us, let the Lord put all their enemies—all death, distress, and pain—under their feet as "a footstool" for them.

To do this, we have to insist on the fixed Good in the terrorist, the thief, and the politician. We have to insist on the fixed Good in the corporate capitalist as well as the philanthropist.

As we do so, difficult as it may be, one distressing idea and experience after another will fade away without our personal effort—even without our mental effort. Each distress will fall by the power of the spoken word and the unspoken certainty that all is, in Truth and deed, Good.

THE METAPHOR

Whoever sees the Good fixed in the universe sees what is meant by the symbol of the white stone as the foundation of the New Jerusalem (new place of peace) described in John's Book of Revelation.[6] The white stone stands for the Good that stays fixed and pure eternally in the universe and remains so regardless of activity around it. Whoever sees that the Good cannot be defeated shall find that the world around them is experiencing the peace and well-being that's symbolized by the white stone.

THE EXPERIENCE

This first lesson has been given many times over to humanity by spiritual teacher after spiritual teacher, sometimes simply, sometimes abstrusely. It tells us that the presence of what the Psalmist calls the Lord speaks in wondrous language to our own ego-self, our intellect, our human mind at its highest intelligence, which has been our lord until now. The continued unspeakable kindness of the Lord, the Indescribable Source of All, is the ongoing nourishment of all life—and so it has been promised to us across faith traditions.

Yet the teaching has always held implications deeper and further than the small ego can understand—that is, until the ego-self has "sat on the right hand" of the Good and has seen the Good fixed in all things.

The ego-self sees this good not with the eyes, nor even with the heart, but by choosing the principles being taught by those who have learned this esoteric Science. This is not an act of blind acceptance nor even of loving compassion; it's a reasoned choice of unchanging principle over constantly shifting perception. When this choice becomes automatic, then the once-limited ego-self becomes the unlimited Higher Self, one with the Oversoul, reasoning not with the limitations of intellect but by the unlimited Principle of Truth.

Think about it: the master teachers haven't given things to, nor even spoken aloud about, the poverty-stricken wretch crying with hunger before them. Instead, with their deeper reasoning, they have simply spoken Truth silently within. With their inner voice, they have said to the hungry one's mind words like, "Because the Good is omnipotent, because the Good is God, kind and bountiful and everywhere present, you cannot be hungry; this experience is not real, now or ever." This manner of secret reasoning conveys a kind of nourishment to the mind that has the power to turn thought into nourishment and the money to buy nourishment. It's the reasoning that turned the widow's one jar of oil into many in the Hebrew Bible story[7] and caused the lame men to walk in the Christian New Testament.[8]

Even those who are not directly present are lifted by the steady, right reasoning of one man or woman who will not agree that want and misery are reality. As the work of psychiatrist David Hawkins demonstrates, people who are operating at a state of consciousness focused on love and unity affect millions of others simply by being aware.[9]

This is why, in every age, someone must know without doubt that the Good that is called God is unconditional loving-kindness surrounding and upholding all the people; it's not partial to princes, kings, capitalists, or priests. The unemployed and distressed masses must have such people holding the Principle of Truth in mind or "sit on the Lord's right hand" for them until they can do it themselves. Someone must do so till the Good that is called God makes all people realize their equality with kings and princes—in both possessions and opportunities. This was the role of the chiefs, priests, shamans, and matriarchs of ancient times, as illustrated in the stories of White Buffalo Woman and King Arthur. This understanding, this speaking the words of the Lord, is the essence of the American Declaration of Independence: that all people are "created equal, that they are endowed by their Creator with certain unalienable Rights, that among these are Life, Liberty and the Pursuit of Happiness."

Learning to focus on the always-present Good, rather than the transient world around us, is a practice that pulls people into positions of leadership. In the Hebrew scriptures, we read of Joseph, the young boy who kept his focus on the God-presence and rose from slavery to "sit at the right hand of" the pharaoh and govern Egypt.[10] In the New Testament, we read of the sisters in Bethany: Mary and Martha. Mary sat listening to their teacher while Martha complained that she wasn't helping to prepare the meal.[11] Sitting still, Mary declared the Truth we set forth here. Seeing that Truth everywhere, she became the "Apostle to the Apostles" and converted the world. Martha, trying to make Mary see how hard life is, how slow the Good is to manifest, did not reign. Her declarations, being contrary to Truth, brought forth all the toil and hardship that's been called evil, and could not stand. Her limited beliefs of what's possible fell into nothingness. Not until she left behind her understanding of how the world works could she come into her power, which she did, according to a tale told by the residents of Provence, France, when she arrived in the town of Tarasque and defeated the fearful monster dwelling there.

Since the Source of All is always providing goodness, each of us can know we are always provided for: food and comfort are as certain for us as beauty is for the rose. They are our unalienable rights.

This fixed Good is always present but will only seem to work swiftly if we see it with conviction in our hearts. It comes to me while

I'm obeying the simple direction of talking and thinking only about the fixed Good, regardless of externals. I experience life, health, strength, support, protection, intelligence, beauty, and power immediately when my talking ego-self wholeheartedly proclaims this first lesson in the Spiritual Science. In this way, the everlasting Principle of Truth reigns. In this way, we become the noble beings we were born to be.

LOOKING WITHIN

A second part of this first lesson is the realization that the Good, or God, that we believed was outside us is, in fact, within each and every being. This is the essence of Taoism: the divine flow enlivens all beings. It's what quantum physics leads us to know as well, as Fred Alan Wolf, William Tillich, and Amit Goswami, authors of several texts in the field, tell us in interviews in the films *What the Bleep Do We Know!?* and *What the Bleep!?: Down the Rabbit Hole.* The underlying energy and intelligence of the quantum field pervades all that is and encourages order, harmony, and balance in the seemingly chaotic processes of the universe—and ourselves.

This was expressed by the great teacher Jesus in the words "the Kingdom of God is within you,"[12] and "Pray unto your Father in heaven."[13] He tells us that the Lord, the Highest Brahman, the Father, the Great Spirit, is in all people alike and teaches us to pray to our own Self. He even gives us the words, which, translated from the Aramaic that the disciples heard, are as follows:

> Give me this day my daily supply. Let me not walk on the side of the hard and the unkind appearance, even when to my eyes and heart it seems so real . . . You, Lord, are my light and my life . . . my salvation . . . You are Great, having Your everlasting presence even in me, ever near for me to call upon . . . I fear no evil, for You are always with me.[14]

Ralph Waldo Emerson expands on this understanding in his essay "Self-Reliance," in which he wrote that the power and authority to become our true selves is not to be found in anything outside of us but in our true Self, our higher nature. To our own God within ourselves, to the highest of ourselves, we shall address ourselves and be free.

True Repentance

Repentance means turning away from what is not Truth toward what is, toward the "I AM," the Brahman, the Lord, the Father at our own center. Then, reasoning from its glory-presence in us, we see its glory in our world. Choosing this principle of Divinity Within, we turn away from expecting some external being to come down and do things for us. This is true repentance.

Repentance means turning from judging your life and character by the human, fearful, lying side and judging it by the divine, eternal side instead. Those who speak of the fixed Good in me and around me are translating from the Lord's instructions into their own lord's speech. Hearing their voices, I turn to behold my Lord within. I am satisfied with myself. I am happy in myself. I see that my own highest Brahman is the Lord. I no longer use the ego-based human nature as the basis for my thought and action.

Thus repenting, I take the miraculous nourishment of seeing my Good, the Lord, everywhere. To me, all are God. This is the true Statement of Being. And so it is for everyone.

Essential Points

- Spiritual Science is based on the understanding that mind affects matter whenever words are spoken aloud or in the mind.
- This Science goes infinitely further than the sciences based on what can be observed with the senses; it's not just physical but *metaphysical*. The term *meta* means beyond, and what is beyond has no limit.
- The first lesson in the various esoteric traditions of the world is that there is One and One only, and we are part of that One and empowered by our place in it.
- Where I focus on the One is only Good—Good that is omnipresent (everywhere, in all things), omnipotent (all the power that is), and omniscient (all-pervading intelligence).

- Whoever understands the idea that Truth is the Good tells that Truth and it will defeat every lie, even every appearance of wrongdoing without their personal effort.
- When the choice to see only the Good becomes automatic, then the once-limited ego-self becomes the unlimited Higher Self, one with the Oversoul, reasoning not with the limitations of intellect but by the unlimited Principle of Truth.
- The second part of this first lesson is the realization that the Good, or God, that we believed was outside us is, in fact, within each and every being.
- Repentance means turning away from what is not Truth toward what is, toward the "I AM" at everyone's own center, turning from judging our life and character by the human, fearful, lying side to judge it by the divine eternal side instead. Reasoning from its glory-presence in us, we then see its glory in our world.

Practicing the Principle

Sit down at a certain time every day and write on a piece of paper what your idea of Good is and the highest ideas of Good that your inner vision holds. This repetition will make it more real, and this process will deepen and clarify your understanding of the Good you seek—and are.

LESSON 2
RETURNING TO OUR TRUE NATURE

When most people hear the statement that "all is One and that One is Good, omnipotent," as in the first lesson, the first thought they have is that it can't be true. Our culture has taught us the idea that there are two aspects of reality, not one, and that there is conflict between two powers. As a result, most people think of reality as a balance of Good and evil; Spirit and matter; Life and death. They have the thought that the omnipotence of Good can't be true, for they've seen evil rampant in the world, in conflict with the goodness of Spirit.

But when they allow themselves to contemplate the idea further, they're inspired to see that in those apparent conflicts, Spirit must prevail, and after the smoke of the seeming battle has cleared away, they see that all is Spirit, as it must be, since Spirit is the substance that forms matter.

This process—inspiration followed by questioning, experiencing conflict, and finally coming to a higher understanding—is the essence of most apocalyptic writings (the Greek word *apocalypse* meaning "lifting the veil"), including John's book of Revelation in the Christian New Testament.

Every first lesson in metaphysics conveys this breath of inspiration. The very word *inspiration* implies a new breath, for like *respiration*, *aspiration*, *expiration*, and even *conspiracy*, it comes from the same root meaning, the Latin word *spiritus*, which translates as "breath, wind, spirit." Our first encounter with a spiritual truth, then, is the inbreathing of a new understanding, a new principle, which permits a new life and everything that follows.

But the mind is like the body in that its expiration is as important as inspiration.

The second lesson of metaphysics, therefore, is expiration, or release. It's the throwing off or refusal of what's not essential or life sustaining. The idea of hate, for example, is neither life sustaining nor essential. Nor is the idea of ignorance. So, with the breath of the mind outward, we let go of these ideas. We are breathing forth from our mind, releasing any ideas not essential or supportive of life—we are expiring them.

In following the invitation of our Lord to "sit on the right hand," we see only our source, guide, and provider. When we do so, we realize that our Lord as Spirit, the Tao, Brahman, Allah, the ground of being, is in everything, everywhere. What we're focusing on and being guided by is the Fundamental Intelligence in the underlying quantum field, the orderly substance of all that is energy and matter.

More and more physicists are beginning to see that the underlying quantum field out of which both matter and energy emerge is almost purely information—and can be thought of as the One that Hindus and Buddhists call Brahman and what we're calling Lord or Spirit. Einstein said matter is energy ($E=mc^2$) and since then, quantum physicists have demonstrated many times over that the fundamental units of the quantum field show up as energy or matter, depending on the circumstances.

Spirit is also energy, but energy that is ordered, informed. Systems theorists say that everything in the universe consists of matter, energy, and information. There's a lot of matter in a pound of lead but not as much energy as a pound of uranium or as much information as in a human brain. The more information there is in something, the more complex its structure, so something can be very complex and highly energetic and yet have very little matter in it, like the memory systems of a cell phone or a molecule-sized nanobot.

Spirit and matter therefore can't be in conflict, since matter is energy taking form according to the information present in Spirit. This means that the world we see is the substance of Spirit made manifest as forms of matter, and whatever forms are not the Good must dissolve as we insist on seeing only the Good that is Truth. As we understand this, we begin to see the world around us as energy and information, as Spirit, rather than as solid matter. "The world is clean dissolved before us, says the Lord."[1]

All the Good we call God, or my Lord, is Spirit, with many names and aspects: Life, Truth, Love, Intelligence, Peace, Harmony, Order, and more. And as we focus on that Good, we begin to see Life everywhere and begin to ignore death. Harmony and Order fill our awareness. We realize that the only death there is, is our own letting go of unessential ideas; the only conflict is our struggle to release that which no longer serves us.

RELEASING AND DISSOLVING

This is a Science that casts out evil, matter, sickness, death, hate, error, and all idea of sin. It's a Science of establishing the kingdom of Spirit by proclaiming that all is Spirit; there is no matter—all is Life; there is no death. It's a Science that never experiences conflict. It is therefore a Science of the expiration of conflict, the Science of negation through denial.

Refusing evil is, in its esoteric or mystic sense, the ministry of destruction. There is no destroyer like the Lord. "I came not to bring peace on earth, but a sword."[2] The sword comes as the archangel Michael, the Hindu destroyer deity Indra (who is actually an aspect of the trinity of Brahman in the same way the Holy Spirit is an aspect of the Christian trinity), or the Buddhist destroyer demon Vajrakilaya to cut away that which no longer serves us.

The ideas of separation, ignorance, and death that form so much of our experience are our ego-self lord at work. The Science of release through denials leads us to see that when we say "there is no evil; all is Good," we are putting out our old ego-self lord and retaining the Lord. That Lord, in one form or another, comes to sweep away all that no longer serves us, all that is no longer vital to us, so we may be free.

It's not vital to look upon evil and death as Good. It is vital to say they do not exist. It is vital to say that there's no conflict between Spirit and matter, for Spirit is all; matter dissolves in our awareness of Spirit as Substance.

The Yaqui shaman Don Juan Matus went to great lengths and used many teaching devices to help his student Carlos Castaneda come to experience this dissolution of solid matter into the energy and spiritual Substance that is really there.[3]

Jesus the Nazarene, speaking the words of the Lord as he heard them, said, "Blessed are the poor in Spirit, for theirs is the Kingdom of Heaven."[4] Jesus saw that to be free from matter, free in the Spirit, is a form of utter poverty, and he called that poverty blessedness. He saw that once inspired, we would all see matter dissolve into Spirit and all that would remain is the One, and in that awareness is the blessed-ness we call Heaven.

In physics, saying that matter is energy helps us see all material objects as forms of energy. In metaphysics, constantly speaking of all as Good and saying there is no evil helps us see the omnipresent Good. Likewise, by constantly speaking that all is Spirit, the omnipresent Spirit comes into view, and we begin to experience that there is no matter where we once felt blocked or hindered by it. At that point the ego-mind stops and the Lord takes the reins of the mind and experience exactly as promised in the psalm we referred to in lesson 1: "I will make your enemies your footstool."[5]

THE POWER OF THE NAME

For everyone, everywhere, there is some name, some image that when we contemplate it, we feel the presence of a higher power for Good working in our lives. For Muslims, the sound of "Allah," or naming the blessed prophet Mohammed is sufficient. Some people invoke a feminine deity or saint, calling on Mary, the blessed Mother of God ("Hail Mary" or Ave Maria), or envisioning Tara or Kali or simply their image of the universal Mother. Others allow their awareness to expand into the vast universe. For Christians, speaking the name "Jesus Christ" (said in whatever language one has spoken since childhood) can evoke that state. Buddhists and Hindus follow the guidance of Krishna to Arjuna in the Bhagavad Gita by repeating the word Om. In the Hebrew Bible, the name "I AM" is synonymous with the Emmanuel presence—and power.

These are not the true Name of the divine, because the true Name is incomprehensible to the human mind, but they bring us closer to understanding and experiencing the presence and power that is everywhere, letting us feel the omnipotent Name even though it's not possible to speak it. "Your Name is an ointment poured forth."[6] "The Name of the Lord is a strong tower."[7]

The mystery of our lives is the state of consciousness that naming our understanding of our Emmanuel, our own eternal "God present to us" (which is what Emmanuel means), brings us into. The Substance of Life enters the body in a new way when the mind breathes in the name Emmanuel, and ideas of death are gone. Ideas of ignorance are gone as well.

The Name of our Emmanuel presence is in everyone. We need not seek it. Everyone lives in an unscalable tower of eternal safety, within a Name that saves. Knowing this, even though we may not be able to say that Name, we never need to know fear.

There is a Love that is beyond letting go of hate. It's the Love that inspires those who inspire others, and it's available in that state of consciousness we experience when we're focusing on the Emmanuel Name.

There is a life that knows no death. It's the life Christians tell us that Jesus the Nazarene embodied and said we would as well when we focus on his Emmanuel presence. It's what prophets and saints of all traditions have all experienced at times in their lives—the experience being what makes them prophets and saints. And they've told us that it's available to all of us once we can sustain that state of consciousness in which the Emmanuel presence is all in all to us. We can all know the deathless life that is our true nature.

THE BREATH OF LIFE

There is a Life beyond even the life that has to let go of death. By breathing the air of the atmosphere into the nose and at the same time drawing into the mind the Name of our Emmanuel, we are taking both mental and physical breaths. The Emmanuel Name has in it a quickening energy. It expels our useless notions with its mystic body, which is within us when we inspire. This is Hawaiian spiritual aloha; it is the Hindu *prana yoga*. So we breathe in.

In the quantum sciences, we are told that a handful of air contains all the energy needed to power a city. So we breathe in.

In the biological sciences, we are told that when we breathe, we are giving our cells the oxygen they need to function properly. So we breathe in.

Then we are told that waste products in the body are released as we exhale. So we breathe out.

But in Spiritual Science, we perceive that there is a Life independent of the physical. It's the metaphysical. Aren't people something beyond inspiration and expiration?

Whoever is independent of breath or belief has achieved a state of consciousness where they can lay down their breath (or life) and take it up again at will. In the Christian tradition, that state is embodied in Jesus the Nazarene, who said, "I lay down my body and take it up at will."[8] Among the Hindus, the highest yogis and saints have demonstrated thousands of times over the centuries that the properly trained person can learn to shut down all physiological processes and start them up at will. Some indigenous traditions tell of shamans who have done the same. And for those who study the Great Pyramid and the Egyptian Book of the Dead carefully, it's clear that the essence of the ancient Egyptian mysteries of immortality is the ability to practice this skill.

THE "I" AT THE CENTER

If we breathe the Emmanuel Name inward, hold the breath, and then let it go, we find at the core of our being a Self that's not mixed up with the breath at all. We discover the "I" of our being, an Intelligence that observes and guides us always. This practice is the essence of contemplative prayer in the Western religious traditions as well as the Sufi and Kabbalist traditions, and is the essence of the Yoga Sutras of Patanjali and other Hindu texts.

There is an intelligence that knows no ignorance. It's that Intelligence that we breathe into our mind by naming our Emmanuel. We name the Name and are inspired. As we focus on the Emmanuel Name, we see our true Self, the true "I," standing back and breathing in and then breathing outward and releasing all that is not Good. We see that the Hindu-Buddhist guru, Jesus the Nazarene, and all twelve Hebrew prophets all understood this process. They taught us to be independent of words through it. Then we realize that, indeed, something is more wonderful than words.

What's more wonderful than spoken words? The "I" that uses them. It's the observer Self of the yogic traditions, the soul-self of the shaman. The Nazarene called this "I" the Father, or in the Aramaic of the time, First Mover. Gautama Buddha called it the Buddha Nature, or Atman. This "I" fathers all things. That is, it starts all things. It's the mystic body of all beings.

It shows us that the Life we call God may quicken us into a state that has no opposite and can be sent forth from our mind to others. It moves the breath of the physical body as air and energy (sometimes called *chi* or *prana*) and the breath of mind as words or ideas.

Whoever sees behind the breaths and behind the thoughts to the starting point of their "I" is one with the highest Self indeed. They are the true mystics. They know that they are Self and God in one.

The "I" at my center stops and starts all breath and thoughts, but is always independent of them. The "I" at my center is my Self. It's what the Hindus call *Atman*, connected with Brahman, upon whom it depends, upon whom it feeds. My ego-self, my intellect, can never comprehend that Self, but the independent unlimited "I" can comprehend all.

The "I" at the center is exposed by breathing in the doctrine of all that is Good (affirming) and breathing out the doctrine that there is no evil (denying). Both kinds of statement are true. One swings the curtain of human experience to the right; the other to the left. One breathes the breath of Truth inward, and the other breathes it outward. There, where the two are parted, stands the exposed center.

If you think it's difficult to say that the "I" that stands at that center must be the one who stops thoughts and sets them going, consider the following: Laying down the book you're reading seems to stop the flow of the information and picking it up seems to revive its information flow. If the body that is sustained by inspiration and expiration of air is really energy, isn't it easy for the "I" who stands at the center of the body and is clothed by it to lay it down? If our less solid body, which we call the mind, is but an appearance sustained by the flow of thoughts that come and go, is it not easy for the "I" at the center to lay the mind down and pick it up again?

If you think it's difficult to say that the "I" at the center of your mind must be that which stops the breath and sets it going again, think about this: when a breather stops breathing, we call it death, yet clearly the "I" controlling the breath stopped it.

No Evil

In this Science, we hold the reasonable idea that there is no pain or discord in our idea of Good. This simple denial of the reality of pain and discord is a statement of Truth, for in omnipresent Good, there *can* be nothing we would call evil.

When we hold the doctrine that all is Good, that there is no evil, regardless of appearances, we are reaching the "I" at the center of our being. And when that "I" "sits on the right hand of the Lord," saying, "All is Good," it must also say, "That which is not Good does not exist."

And when that happens, the "I" that governs our experience can bring forth only good experiences: pain and discord are no longer part of our experience or world. So we affirm the Good and deny the existence of evil.

Following this line of reasoning further, all the apparently evil sights and sounds of our daily observations are the result of stopping the thoughts of our "I" from guiding our experience. We do so by repressing our true thoughts, the breath of the mind, holding them inward. Suppose you see someone beating a dog. It's the result of your stopping the thought of peace flowing from the "I" at your center. Let that thought flow free again and see how peaceful the dog will feel, how peaceful the person will feel, how still the hand will be. In all situations, let the thoughts of the "I" flow freely again, and see how the world becomes a heaven.

Expiring Death, Inspiring Immortality

The religions of humanity have long declared that all of us shall live in, with, and as Everlasting Divinity forever. They tell us that whoever sees God/Brahman/Goddess *is* the divine Good. The histories of the world's religions remind us that whoever sees the divine Omnipotence performs divine works. They tell us that wherever these people breathe their breaths of inspiration and expiration, Good appears; that is, wherever they think their true thoughts, Good appears.

Such people know that whatever seems evil is only their mental breath drawn inward, blocking the thoughts of God. Letting that breath go free again, peace and joy and light and life are shed across the planet.

They know that whatever seems evil in the world is only their blocked thoughts returning in form. Letting those thoughts go again, freely over the earth, they see only light, joy, peace, intelligence.

Seeing Only Good

These people, focusing their attention on the divine Good, realize that the denials of Science have a powerful purpose. By negating the possibility of evil, by turning only to the Good, they see what is truly real.

Looking toward their Father-Mother-God, their Great Spirit, their Brahman, the "I" transcending their ego-self, they see only the Good that is omnipresent, and they never see less than that. They see that, in the fact that they are the "I" at the center, they are lord over all the earth. They see that they are the divinity who breathes into the creature (their own body) the breath of life, or withdraws breath—at free choice.

Essential Points

- When people first consider the statement that "all is One and that One is Good, omnipotent" most of them have the thought that it can't be true, for they've seen evil rampant in the world, in conflict with the goodness of Spirit.
- The second lesson of metaphysics is expiration, or release. It's the throwing off or refusal of what's not essential or supportive of life, such as a belief in lack or a past hatred.
- The world we see is the Substance of Spirit made manifest as forms of matter, and whatever forms are not the Good must dissolve as we insist on seeing only the Good that is Truth.
- This is a Science that casts out evil, matter, sickness, death, hate, error, and all idea of sin. It's a Science of establishing the kingdom of Spirit by proclaiming that all is Spirit; there is no matter—all is Life; there is no death.
- For everyone, everywhere, there is some name, some image that when we contemplate it, we feel the presence of a higher power for Good working in our lives.
- The Emmanuel ("God present to us") Name is in everyone. We need not look for it. Everyone lives in an unscalable tower of eternal safety. Knowing this, we never need to know fear.
- The "I" at my center is my Self. My ego-self, my intellect, can never comprehend that Self, but the independent unlimited "I" can comprehend all.
- When that "I" "sits on the right hand of the Lord," saying, "All is Good," it must also say, "That which is not Good does not exist."

• Those who realize this know that whatever seems evil in the world is only their own blocked thoughts returning in form. Letting those thoughts go again, they see only light, joy, peace, intelligence.

Practicing the Principle

1. Each day, lift your vision to the One that is the Source of All and acknowledge the Truth: that as Good is omnipresent, you reject the common feeling of the absence of Good. As the Everlasting One is free, you are free. Now. Sing the joy of liberty, free grace, remission, and unburdening.

   If it helps to have a set of statements to repeat, use the following (you may even wish to make up a tune and sing it):

• Steadfastly focusing on the One that is my Source, there is no evil, discord, nor distress on my pathway.
• Steadfastly focusing on the One that is my Source, there is no matter with laws to limit me, but all is Spirit, supporting my bliss.
• Steadfastly focusing on the One that is my Source, there is no loss, lack, or absence—no deprivation of any kind.
• Steadfastly focusing on the One that is my Source, there is nothing to fear anywhere, as there is no hurtful thing and no power that can hurt me.
• Steadfastly focusing on the One that is my Source, there is neither sin nor sickness nor death in my world.

2. Set aside an afternoon and go somewhere where you can be alone and where any noise you make will not disturb others, to discover what ideas about yourself and divinity you have held in the past that no longer serve you. They may be ideas about having to work or strive to experience Good. They may be ideas about illness or death having more power than Good. They may be ideas about others having more power than you or you having more power, knowledge, or skill than others.

a. Accept that these ideas no longer serve you or your world. Acknowledge that they've brought you to the place where you are, and now they have served their purpose and may be left behind. Appreciate their usefulness in the past, and pay attention to the feelings that come up as you do so. Write down those feelings and allow them to flow. Express your joys and fears and anger by moving your body as feels appropriate and saying the words you've written aloud, knowing that no one is harmed by your expressing your feelings in a safe space.

b. Keep expressing until there's nothing left and you feel drained. Then burn or shred the paper you've been writing on, releasing these ideas and all the incidents and people that supported them. Imagine the ideas you've been releasing being transformed by the fire or the shredder and all the feelings you've expressed being lifted by a rocket into the sun to become healing light for all.

c. At that point, allow yourself to feel the love that is truly there for all the people who've been part of these ideas. Imagine them in front of you, singly or as a group, and tell them all you have to say, and then listen. Even in your inner world, the people in your life may surprise you with what they have to say about their role in your life. As you listen, you'll feel a warm light flooding your being. Let that light surround you and them, enfolding you all with love. Be the love and claim it as the Truth of your relationships with these people.

d. In that love, claim the Good that is always present. Name the perfect idea that you're ready to live by instead of the one that you've released. Claim it and write it down. Post it somewhere that will remind you of it when your old habit of thought seems to take over.

e. Now congratulate yourself; you've transformed your mind!

LESSON 3
THE HUNGRY CATERPILLAR

Why is there such an appearance of hunger everywhere? Why is everyone longing to fill themselves with something other than what they already have?

This is humanity's caterpillar state. The caterpillar must always be gnawing on everything in sight, until it finally discovers its true body. So we humans continue to hunger and gnaw until we finally discover the "I" at our center that we explored in the previous lesson. Then, like the caterpillar which, when it has given up constantly gnawing, can rest and become its true form, we, too, can rest and become our true Self.

Can anyone believe that the Source of All That Is seeks more? If not, then if I am seeking more, my mind and body are in the caterpillar condition, and the Lord at my center is not known to me—even if I preach great doctrine and make myself famous for great knowledge of God. For if the Lord, the Source of All That Is, would not seek for more, how could I know the Lord and still seek for more?

The eating practice of the body is called *feeding*. The eating practice of the mind is called *prayer* or *affirmation*. Both, while supportive of human well-being, are wholly ungodly; they are not the activities of the "I" in us but of our ego-selves, believing that we are not, or have not,

29

enough. They are a sign that we feel separated from our Good, which cannot be true, since what we call God, as Good, is omnipresent.

And experience of the Good never requires sacrifice or suffering. Let no one believe that feeding their body with sufferings would cause them to find the un-hungry God, by whatever Name, or the "I" they already own, the "I Am" of their being.

When people talk of certain actions they must perform and of certain actions they must not perform, they are being a hungry caterpillar. When anyone speaks of certain thoughts they must focus on and of certain ones they must never think, they are a caterpillar hungering after their un-hungry "I Am" by gnawing on thoughts. They do not make this gnawing more divine by calling it philosophy or contemplation or what Theosophists call *raja yoga*.

There's an ancient story that Simeon of Antioch perched on a tower sixty feet high for thirty-seven years. An iron chain around his neck caused his forehead to touch his feet. His caterpillar nature longed for suffering to appease its deeper hunger—to experience the "I" at his center. As this amount of suffering did not satisfy, he added further tortures. He took only two meals per week. This is abuse of the body trying to find the "I" that needs nothing. It's called asceticism and is contrary to the nature of the "I" it seeks.

It does not spiritualize this caterpillar performance to call it penance or yoga. When Prince Gautama chose to leave the luxuries of his palace life, he entered the forest and became an ascetic, practicing the most extreme forms of yoga. For years he suppressed the body, depriving it of food, shelter, even the cleansing waters of the river, sitting for countless hours in lotus position, seeking peace and the end of suffering. Then one day, he realized that the body and mind need no such sufferings to achieve peace. He swam in the river, ate some of his favorite food, rested under the Bodhi tree, and was enlightened. Then he sat in joyful freedom for forty days, free of the need for food or any other form of satisfaction, as he contemplated the Truth he had discovered.

The day we cease to seek more, that day we are one with our Source and are far out of the reach of calamity.

RESTORATION

That day sometimes seems far off. But fortunately there is a promise that assists us: "I will restore to you the years that the locusts [caterpillar] hath eaten."[1] Because of this promise, I lose nothing and no time by eating or shopping, though I should spend a million years feeding myself or acquiring goods. I lose no time by thinking. I lose no divinity by thinking and thinking, even if I spent a million years thinking. For, in the moment that I recognize my Lord, the years the caterpillar has eaten are suddenly restored, no matter what I have done or said or thought.

Restoration cannot take place where something is lost. The very word *restoration* shows that the something was always there to be laid hold of. So nothing is ever lost. In fact, nothing is ever gained. The Lord restores what we thought we had lost, and now it is as it already was.

The great Hebrew king and poet Solomon proclaimed that there never had been anything new and never would be anything new. What is now is all there ever was and ever will be. The Nazarene said plainly that nothing can be added to or taken from the "I," which he called the Father. Therefore, nothing said against anyone gives them any hurt— and nothing said *for* people gives them any good. In Truth, they are what they are in reality, whole and complete; they always were what they are; they always will be what they are. Nothing we or they do or say can change that. They are Almighty God, Brahman: untouchable, unstoppable.

SATISFACTION

The ego-self gnaws to feel satisfied and indestructible, trying to be like the almighty "I." But since the almighty "I" never gnaws to get inde-structible, it's plain that gnawing, struggling, taking, or fighting will not lead to the satisfied "I."

In the various natural and social sciences, people are gnawing, struggling to discover that which already exists. They collect data and then they work it over into "new" combinations and structures that already exist somewhere.

In Spiritual Science, we are discovering life that already exists both in essence and in manifest form. Then we say that all beings have all the life there is. We lay hold of health that already exists and we say that everyone already owns all the health there is. We lay hold of strength that already exists, and we say that everyone already owns all the strength there is.

In the previous lesson, we saw that regardless of form or language, the Name of the Lord, our Emmanuel, is eternal ointment, eternal safety. But no one can speak that Name—only names that bring us closer to It—so everyone keeps the saving Name of the Lord unspoken, untold, unthought. They keep it where they are not hungry, at that central "I" of their being.

Both mind and body are temporal, unreal, while the majestic "I Am," the "I" of our being, is eternal Substance, always nourished, never hungry. This eternal I Am Substance is by itself. It's not identified with anything, yet is the eternal cause of all, in the same way that the sun is the cause of the grass, yet is never identified with the grass.

Likewise the mind that gnaws hungrily shall be filled with the fiery "I Am" nature, that glory, that inspiration. But it's not by gnawing and eating that satisfaction occurs; rather, it's by turning and looking. Just as the plant turns toward the sun and is beautified, the body and mind, with their hungry gnawing, turn to look at the divine "I Am," and it shines so wondrously through them that they are beautiful.

They may even be transfigured. There is a way of inner eyesight, the mind's eye turning backward and upward toward the I Am, till it never has to speak or think for itself. The original un-hungry, shining I Am streams in radiance through it till there is no reasoning mind whatever. The body-mind is transfigured into the light of the I Am.

Krishna said, "With their minds and lives entirely absorbed in Me, enlightening each other and always speaking of Me, they are satisfied and delighted."[2] The prophet Isaiah said, "Look unto Me and be ye saved, all the ends of the earth."[3] The mind's eye can turn to the One with the

Name that cannot be spoken, and we experience the thoughts and feelings parting, this way and that, like opening doors. Then, suddenly, down through that opening, unspeakable glory descends, and the un-hungry Lord fills the being. Those doors are now wide as Heaven and can no longer be shut, forever. The darkest, most heavily weighted mind may turn and look toward that One, and suddenly, all its weights are gone; it is now an open doorway and all inspiration soars in splendor through it.

The hunger of the eyes to see is a sign of there being something to see, and that something, being seen, is all that remains. The hunger of the ears to hear is a sign that there is something to hear, and that something, being heard, is all there is of us. The hunger of the hands to touch and the tongue to taste are signs of there being an Original One to touch and taste, and, when they have touched and tasted, there is nothing for them but That.

Turn back! Turn in repentance! Why play the caterpillar when the "I Am" is ever-present and All?

Essential Points

- Humanity is like a hungry caterpillar, gnawing at everything in sight while it seeks true, spiritual nourishment.
- The eating practice of the body is called *feeding*. The eating practice of the mind is called *prayer* or *affirmation*. Neither is the activity of the "I" of us, but of our ego-selves, believing that we are not, or have not, enough.
- When people talk of certain actions that they must perform or not perform, they are being a hungry caterpillar. When anyone tells of certain thoughts they must focus on or must never think, they are a caterpillar hungering after their un-hungry "I Am."
- The day we cease seeking more, that day we are one with our Source and are far out of the reach of calamity.
- What is now is all there was and ever will be. Nothing said against anyone gives them any hurt; nothing said for people gives them any good. In Truth, they are whole and complete; they always were; they always will be. Nothing we or they do or say can change that.

- In Spiritual Science, we say that all beings have all the life there is, that everyone already owns all the health there is, and everyone already owns all the strength there is.
- The mind's eye can turn to the One with the Name that cannot be spoken and experience the thoughts parting, like doors opening. Then, suddenly, down through that opening, unspeakable glory descends, and the un-hungry Lord fills the being, and those doors can no longer be shut forever.

Practicing the Principle

Every night, before going to sleep, give glad, joyous praises to the Most High Source of all that is, acknowledging that the Holy Spirit fills your thoughts with power and passion for Truth and fires your affairs to splendid achievements.

Every morning, as you prepare for the day, wash away any thoughts of disease or distress and fill your mind with the Emmanuel Name that empowers, and thoughts of the Good that you are experiencing.

LESSON 4
CONFIDENCE OF MIND

When the hypnotist whispers to me that an onion is an orange, which part of me agrees and which sits serenely, independent of the hypnotist? What is the "I" of me?

While you're sleeping, you're in the midst of your own inner world, but are you in the world we call sleep? While you dream, are you not aware that all that's happening happens to you and you are never that which happens? Even if it seems close, don't you still feel that, though in the dream, you are not of it?

What is this you that's never anything that happens? What is this which is able to leave the panorama of every experience behind you and draw it aside from you, no matter how much attention you've given it? Does your attention on a thing make you that thing?

THE UNSEEN SELF

All lessons of metaphysics point to the experience of One and One only. Consider the denials and affirmations we have gathered from the books of the sages of all ages that are repeated in Louise Hay's *Heal Your Life*, Eddy's *Science and Health with Key to the Scriptures*, countless self-help books and CDs, and my own earlier works. They're all calculated to draw us more and more closely to the point of asking what the body of knowledge beyond knowledge may be—what the One that is Source of All may be.

Perhaps all the metaphysics of all times might be summarized as the process of clothing and unclothing that unseen Self. Am I not superior to my clothes? Even if I make my clothes my chief focus in life, I care more for myself than I do for my clothes, for it is myself I clothe. Following this line of reasoning, the honored sages of the world—of China, Arabia, India, Egypt, and elsewhere—came to understand that they were superior to and different from their experiences of Soul.

Concentrating the mind upon concealed objects till they expose themselves has so far exposed only the clothes of the soul. Yet no one is ready yet to say that soul is the final body we all are looking for.

The Hindu priests taught that they were seeking the Self that never grows old or changes, the one that never thinks or desires, the one that never heard of loving, the Being that never heard or spoke of Truth. One might ask: what is the good of seeking for the Self that never ages or decays? Well, you know that it is the push of every being to find the best, that which is free and in bliss. As the stars move on to their points in the heavens, so every being moves on to its bliss.

THE POWER OF WILL

The operations of nature are the clothing of humanity's will. Ralph Waldo Emerson taught this idea in his lectures and essays.[1]

Destiny is the clothing of the mind. This is the essence of Emerson's essay "Spiritual Laws" and most of the prosperity and abundance books that have followed, from James Allen's *As a Man Thinketh* to Wallace Wattles's *The Science of Getting Rich* to Rhonda Byrne's *The Secret*.

When someone's will has confidence in itself, it finds all nature—both within the body and around it—obedient to its command. When someone's mind has confidence in itself, it finds destiny responding to its command. When someone's soul has confidence in itself, it's free from both nature and destiny.

This is what *A Course in Miracles* calls the "order problem," reminding us that what happens to the body is a function of mind, and what happens in mind is a function of the soul, which is the current state of the individualized spirit, or Self, and is beyond the cares of the body and its world.

Understand that the terms *soul*, *mind*, *spirit*, and *will* are all names used by metaphysicians to express their estimate of the being we call the Self.

The word we use to describe the Highest Being defines our experience. When someone calls their God, which is not a being but a quality or set of qualities that creates the beingness of all things, by the name Soul, they are full of loving-kindness and warmth; to that person, God is Life. When mystics speak of God as Spirit, they are free and unburdened; to them, God is freedom from the clothing we call flesh. When someone calls their God by the name Mind or Intelligence, they are clothed with knowledge, and we who observe are astonished at their right "knowledge." Their memory, their understanding, and their judgment spring forth through every movement, word, and look. When someone calls their understanding of God Substance, there is a substantial quality about their character, their possessions, even their words. When someone calls the Highest Being Omnipresence, they diffuse and spread themselves through the Universe. When someone calls the One Omnipotence, they feel their own powerfulness. When anyone calls their God Omniscience, they show great wisdom.

CONFIDENCE

In Spiritual Science, then, what we call mind, will, Soul, and Spirit are all the omnipresent Source that people call God, and thus all confidence of mind and soul is the confidence of the omnipotent Beingness we call God. This confidence is called faith.

It's a great joy for the mind to discover that it compels nature, destiny, body, and action of every kind by its own thoughts. For all practical purposes we could deal only with our mind and its thoughts and, by simple contemplation, compel everything to obey our decrees.

This is the delight described in the book and video *The Secret*. It's the essence of the Emerald Tablet and the science of Alchemy. It's the kind of confidence that knows that when we flip a switch, the light will come on, and when we step on the brake, the car will stop. This confidence can be applied to more and more aspects of our experience until the world around us is transformed to a kind of paradise.

The writers of both the Hebrew and Christian Bibles are, for the most part, dealing with this mind of ours that has the ability to handle material things without appearing to touch them. The Hebrew prophet Eliphaz quoted the well-known law: "You shall decree a thing and it shall be established unto you."[2]

But in dealing steadily with the mind, we discover another intelligence superior to mind, and when we do so, we grant that superior intelligence the right of way in our lives. It's the intelligence we've been calling the Self.

Experiencing the power and bliss of Self, we gladly call the mind we used for making decrees nonexistent, nothing. And at that moment we enter the realm of Pure Awareness, what the Hindus call *sat-chit-ananda*—love-bliss consciousness.

HEALING THE SICK

James, the brother of Jesus the Nazarene, called faith a healing quality of mind. "Faith shall save the sick."[3]

When you pray for your friend to be cured, you are using your mind. At a certain point, you have confidence that your friend will be cured. This confidence is a living, bracing tonic in the atmosphere. Your friend received your confidence and revived. This prayer is not the activity of the "I" but is nonetheless effective.

If we then undertake to explain the state of mind that cures the sick, people declare that it is faith. But if you'd never looked upon the friend in the first place as sick, then you wouldn't have had to raise your confidence.

Have you ever heard of people agonizing in prayer till they saw it was useless to go any further, for they saw that their friend would never get well this side of the grave? Do you think they saw the reality of that friend's life? Didn't they simply see the limit of their own mind and not spring beyond it? Didn't they decide that sickness had a power that was stronger than prayer?

When people experience being sick, their mind causes the experience. This is not how we normally think of sickness, but it's more and more what the biological sciences are finding in their research results. Organic gardeners understand this: if a plant has a pest or disease, they know it's because the plant has been weakened in some way to attract and encourage rather than repel that pest or disease—so they strengthen the plant. Likewise for the human body, if the body is infected with one of the many bacteria it constantly encounters, it's not the bacteria that's the problem; it's the weakened state of the body that can't repel the bacteria. This is why antibiotics may eliminate the bacteria but don't restore the body to health.

According to modern biologists, particularly in the field of psycho-neuroimmunology, the body is weakened in two ways: by overburdening it with inappropriate activity or input, or by stressing it with anxious or angry thoughts. Both are functions of the mind. The mind chooses the activities and inputs, and it chooses the thoughts it focuses on. Moreover, as Louise Hay documents in her book *You Can Heal Your Life*, someone's image of themselves as ill or well can affect their ability to maintain a healthy body. And as *A Course In Miracles* tells us, sickness is one of the ways the ego-self keeps us thinking we are limited and separated from our Good—it's a defense that we use when we feel attacked.[4]

Clearly then, disease and misfortune are not something to prevail over. In reality, as we learned in lesson 2, they cannot and do not exist in omnipresent Good. So what makes disease and misfortune seem to be real? The small ego-self; the human mind.

The human mind draws on the Spiritual Substance within itself to form a body that it calls flesh, and it has the same ability to change the forms it has clothed itself in. This means that all your mind needs to do in order to "change its clothes," to change your body's current form, is to rouse its confidence that it can do so.

Likewise for your friends: when you see them as sick, your mind sees their mind's opinion and activity. But if you draw on your confidence in their wellness to strike off the chains of their sickness, you may see them free of sickness. Yet in doing so, you're only engaging in a mental fight with them, and whoever is strongest will win. This is what much of what is called *faith healing* actually is.

Mental healing, however, is not forcing one mind's will on another. In fact, all treatments in mental healing are processes for removing the ego-self or mortal mind. Does the mind capable of talking about sickness resemble the higher Intelligence beyond it that never knows sickness? True Faith Healing is simply your mind opening itself to see the true state—the whole and perfect Self, the "I"—of your friends, and inviting them to do so also.

This is where the division of mind into mortal (human ego-self) and immortal (divine "I") is made.

TRUE MIND BEYOND EGO-MIND

Who is that Being standing at your center that never sees chains or distress? Does that Being perceive any thing, any form in all its variations, at all? Spiritual Science calls that Being that does no manufacturing of human conditions *Higher Self*, *Higher Power*, *Immortal Mind*, *Immortal Will*, *Immortal Spirit*, and *Immortal God*.

The mortal mind or ego-self, based on the ideas and beliefs it holds about itself and what it calls God, makes all the forms of matter and energy that we can sense and measure.

The mortal mind of the ego-self sees and talks of sickness and lack through its instruments, the tongue and senses. It formulates all deformities, all ugliness, all appearances of lack or distress. It also sometimes formulates beautiful objects and the solutions to the problems it creates, but it is never the central fire, the unseen Reality.

The mind that manufactures prosperity, though often called our Higher Power or God, is also mortal mind. Poverty and prosperity are the clothing the mortal mind formulates for itself. When the mortal mind stretches itself to cure poverty and feels that it will never win, we may see that its confidence in the Immortal Mind that is looking through it, wholly oblivious of the poverty, it is not roused at all.

FAITH AND WORKS

All faith is the confidence of the mortal mind either in itself or in what is Real but out of sight, not perceivable. It's called true Faith when mortal mind does nothing. When the mortal mind stands apart, the less it knows, the less it speaks, the less it acts, and the more visible Immortal Mind in all of us becomes. So the whole aim of metaphysical practice, as far as faith and works is concerned, is to rouse our confidence to the level where mortal mind breaks open for Immortal Mind to gleam through.

The command from the first chapter of Genesis, "Let there be a firmament in the waters," means "Let there be a firm mind in the chaos." It's the command to a shifting, changing, fleeting set of thoughts to let another mind be clearly seen. This is the command that we often make to our own ego-self, our mortal mind, when we tell it to be still.

Whoever stills the ego-self, the mortal mind, finds the changeless, undeviating Mind. Then they get the results of obeying their own Higher Power, their Immortal Self. They find their very body permeated and diffused with that Mind. It is the All to them. Then all things are well with them. Their body becomes healthier, their relationships become more satisfying, and their work is more meaningful and effective. Several decades of research on the physiological and emotional effects of various forms of relaxation, meditation, and visualization have demonstrated this.[5]

When anyone rises to the intensity of saying, "Your will be done," instead of holding strongly to their ego-self will, the curtains of their mortal mind part and fade for the mighty Will of Immortal Mind to be made visible on their path. As we experience this process, we call it faith. We may say that we have confidence that great good is coming to us. When we have a greater degree of faith, we become independent of good or ill, resting in the knowledge that All is Well.

IN THE WORLD BUT NOT OF IT

The Immortal Mind knows no opposites. Mortal mind, intellect, or ego-self, also called Adam-mind, sees and names both good and evil. The compassionate heart, also called Joshua-mind or the "I," sees and names good only. The Higher Self, Goddess Within, Tao, Christ-mind, or Buddha-nature—whatever It may be called, names are neither good nor evil.

The Adam-mind speaks from common sense and with fair reasoning on the question of easy and difficult, sick and well. It judges and evaluates based on the cultural norms and the rules of intellect. In the Exodus story, when the Israelites were preparing to cross over into Canaan, the Joshua-mind found only grapes growing on the plains where the Adam-mind said that giants with menacing faces dwelled there.

Yet Immortal Mind of the Higher Self ignores the grapes and the giants both. It knows that good and evil are only appearances that one may put on or leave off. This is the Buddha-nature, the Christ-mind— that which is in the world but not of it.

The great fifteenth-century yogi saint Babaji kept himself always at the age of sixteen years by never letting the mortal mind speak. He taught that the wise one, instead of aiming to acquire knowledge, should avoid knowledge. He saw how the thoughts of mortal mind are full of creative, formulating power, while in the Immortal Mind all is finished and nothing has to be made.

NONACTION: A CONSCIOUS CHOICE OF FAITH

Understanding this, one realizes that choosing not to act is the source of all power.

Moses caught sight of this when he said in the book of Genesis that all things were created perfect and existed before they appeared upon the earth. This is Plato's "unseen ideal" and theoretical physicist David Bohm's "implicate order." This is the essence of the Tao.

This fourth lesson of Spiritual Science shows that what Moses was speaking of, the Creative Mind, the Immortal Self, is not identified with flesh and blood nor with mortal mind that forms them. That which said "Let there be" was superior to that which obeyed: the outer world whose whole nature is obedience.

In truth, mortal mind, with all its formulations of body and world, is nothing. It's unreal. It seems to itself to be something strong and mighty, but it's entirely unseen by the Intelligence that is in and through all—it's not the Self we seek.

Those who observe this truth experience the absolute freedom from human experiences that religion is expected to bring.

RELIGION AND FAITH

The remnants of twelve great religious systems remain on the earth, all having nearly identical descriptions of their God as the unchangeable, firm Eternal Mind, which our mortal mind falters at the sight of. They are:

- Egyptian or *huna* practices;
- the Hindu faiths of India, which are the ancient Brahmanism polished and refined, including Sikhism and Jainism;
- Buddhism, a later form of Brahmanism lifted into the abstraction of Pure Awareness;
- the religion of Persia, the Zoroastrianism of the Parsi;
- the Hebrew religion, which is called Judaism, including those who study the Kabbalah;
- the Celtic or Wiccan traditions;
- the two Chinese religions: Taoism, and the doctrine of Confucius;
- the philosophical systems of Pythagoras, Socrates, Plato, and Aristotle;
- the various denominations of Christianity; and

- Islam, which is the Arabian religion, the followers of Mohammed, and includes Sufism.

All these religions, which are the background of Spiritual Science, describe faith as the firm quality of mind that stands and sees what, to all sensation and to all appearances from history and circumstances, is impossible. It sees the hidden fruit and throws the visible husks aside.

They all describe the ego-self or mortal mind as the semblance and claim of infinite Intelligence without origin and without substance. They tell us that we must stand aside when challenged and let the warrior within us fight all our battles.

This "we" that is to stand aside they call the ego, sometimes the lord of life and sometimes carnal man. Judeo-Christian scriptures call it carnal man or Satan. Modern fundamentalists call it "the enemy." The early Spiritual Scientists called it mortal mind.

Sadly the religions of the world have not yet been understood so that the freedom people seek can be demonstrated. Too often, when people speak of God, they mean the ego-self lord of their life which rules them. Thus they describe a changeable, arbitrary taskmaster that is not real. These prevalent descriptions of Immortal Mind with an unreliable kindness and perverse cruelty have caused mortal mind to stop far short of opening the doors to reveal the "I" at the center. This understanding of what they call God blocks the firm Mind of the changeless Source and Sustainer of All, whose Name is beyond God, from their experience.

As a result, religion offers mental changes, and we're taught to expect quickening and illumination by these mental changes—but change isn't the same as construction or transformation. It's not the new birth or enlightenment we seek.

Nor can it lead to the Ascension that the Nazarene promised. "We shall not all die; but we shall all be changed," said the Christian apostle Paul[6] early on the path of this Science. But Paul had to go further, into the next level. Then, in later years, it came: "Be ye transformed by the renewing of your mind."[7] This transformation is the result of the firm Mind's clear sight of the Indestructible One.

Practicing Faith

Spiritual Science teaches the ego-self mortal mind how to open the doors of feelings and thoughts to bring about its own departure so the Mind that is real may be realized.

In Buddhism, this is practiced as meditation, whether it be mindfulness or emptiness.

In Confucianism, relinquishing personal desire in favor of the greater good provides the means.

The Hindus practicing yoga call all mind, all will, all destiny and human conditions "clothing," "robes," "bonds," and "bands." They strive to burst these bonds and call it "escaping from themselves." In fact, they seek freedom from the things that fold around them so closely as to seem to become them.

The Muslims practice denying gods, by which they mean mortal mind, and affirming God, by which they mean Immortal Mind, saying, "There is no god but God."

The Buddhists deny the god of their understanding that they may affirm the highest, imperceptible God. "From the highest state of Brahma to the lowest straw, all is delusion."[8]

In the Hebrew tradition Moses said, "Let there be a firmament in the midst of the waters."[9] There is one Substance that stands as the body of all the robes of delusion. That is the firmament of the universe. The "waters" of mind and emotions must be divided, parted, so that the "firmament," the firm Mind, may appear. Then Faith is our norm.

An affirmation is a statement of faith. The higher our affirmations, the wider open the mortal mind divides itself and the more the firmament, the one Substance, can be our experience. In the metaphysics of Aristotle, this Substance is called Energy. The highest affirmations we can make express the most energy. They make it impossible for the mortal mind to even claim to exist.

The affirmations and negations of Spiritual Science quicken and hasten the ego-self mind toward giving up all that it claims to see, to allow an experience of what it does not see. This is what the Christian apostle Paul meant when he said, "Faith is the substance of things hoped for, the evidence of things not seen."[10]

Essential Points

- All lessons of metaphysics drive to the experience of One and One only, the process of clothing and unclothing the unseen Self.
- When someone's will has confidence in itself, it finds all nature obedient to its command. When someone's mind has confidence in itself, it finds destiny responding to its command. When someone's soul has confidence in itself, it's free from both nature and destiny.
- When you pray for your friend to be cured, at a certain point you have confidence that your friend will be cured—the confidence we call faith. When you experience the cure, your friend has received your confidence and revived.
- But if the friend were looked upon in the first place as never sick, then you would not have had to raise your confidence. True faith is simply our mind opening itself to see the true state—the whole and perfect Self—of your friend.
- Disease, misfortune, and lack are not something to prevail over because in reality, in omnipresent Good, they cannot and do not exist. They are formulations of the ego-self or mortal mind.
- According to modern biologists, the body is weakened in two ways: by overburdening it with inappropriate activity or input or by stressing it with anxious or angry thoughts. The mind chooses the activities and inputs, and it chooses the thoughts it focuses on, so it is the cause of the body's illness.
- Whoever stills the ego-self or mortal mind obeys the Self. They find their very body permeated and diffused with that Mind. Then all things are well with them.
- Not to act is the source of all power; this is the essence of the Tao and also Moses's commands.
- Spiritual Science teaches the ego-self, mortal mind, how to bring about its own departure so the Mind that is real may be realized in our experience.

- The affirmations and negations of Spiritual Science quicken and hasten the ego-self mind toward giving up all that it claims to see, to allow an experience of what it does not see.

Practicing the Principle

1. Once a week, look into your life. Look it over and see what you appear to lack. Then tell the highest Truth you can about it and be firm. Write down what you've said and look at it next week to see what has changed.
2. Throughout the day, if you encounter upset, discord, or distress, repeat, "I do not believe in a mixture of good and evil in the world, or in myself. All is Good." Say it with increasing vehemence until you feel its Truth.
3. At night, take your biggest challenge and put some denial and affirmation before it. Then stand firm. Regardless of appearances, hold to your statements. This builds your character and faith. If you need a generic statement to repeat, try saying, "I believe that my God is now working with me to make my Self omnipresent, omnipotent, and omniscient. I believe only in the Good as ruling in my life. I have the Faith of God."

LESSON 5
POWER AND PRESENCE

Whoever shows you how to get acquainted with your Emmanuel presence, to dissolve your ego-self into the divine light of the Absolute, is giving you two or three statements of the Spiritual Science doctrine—and may indeed be giving you all of them. An example of such a teaching might be the "I" that thinks and talks becomes the Absolute when it communes with the Absolute; it becomes the Absolute when it thinks of the Absolute; it dissolves for the Absolute to be all in all.

TWELVE STATEMENTS ACROSS TRADITIONS

There are only twelve statements in Spiritual Science, and they are present in all sacred writings. While there are multitudes of ways to express these twelve statements, the power of the whole twelve may be expressed in one statement: the power is not the words but what comes through the words.

This is why a Christian like Peter may convert three thousand people by one sermon. It's how a diminutive mystic like Mohandas Gandhi can lead a nation into independence from the world's greatest empire and become a saint (a *Mahatma*) in the process: the power of Truth comes through the words we speak.

The first chapter of Genesis in the Hebrew Bible gives us this order, and so does the whole of the gospel of John in the Christian New Testament:

1. *The foundation premise:* There is only God, called "The Word."
2. The denial of the reality of all but God, called "Remission."
3. The affirmation of all as Good, called "Salvation."
4. The firmness of mind in Truth, called "Faith."
5. The work of mind having faith, called "Works."
6. The understanding that illuminates mind when talking and thinking of God, called "Wisdom."
7. The healing of belief in separation and denial of the reality of lust and sensual appetites; acceptance that all is in the One, called "Generation."
8. The denial of appearances and deception, disallowance of outer influences, and accepting only one influence, one informer that is God, called "Light."
9. The rejection of the idea of sin, since Good is all, called "Holiness."
10. The true creation manifest, the exposure of health when truth is told to mind, called "Jerusalem."
11. The denial of foolishness and ignorance in omnipresent Omniscience, called "Judgment."
12. Appreciation for the perfect creation of the One as it becomes manifest everywhere, called "Praise."

The Hindu sages have expressed twelve thoughts that shall heal the world in their philosophy. We have these lessons taken from a little book of raja yoga in the English language, translated from the Sanskrit by the Theosophists, as follows:

1. Brahman, the ground of being, is the all-pervading One.
2. Atman is the Omnipresent principle: the whole formulated world is Atman and nothing but Atman.

3. Sitting in a solitary place being free of desire, curbing passions and meditating on the identification of one's self with that Atman who is One, there is no distinction of place, things, and time—I am Brahman.

4. As the identity and unification of one's self and Atman is known, the belief that oneself is body, senses, and so forth, vanishes and one sees that undivided and indivisible Atman that is the whole world.

5. People become that on which they persistently think because the meaning of Brahman is "the Ever-Create" and as we are that, we constantly create through the focus of our thought.

6. All this universe, visible and invisible, the seer, the seen, and the sight, are one eternal consciousness. Those who become enlightened, through their mind, will be ever filled with the bliss of identifying with universal consciousness.

7. Only those people who are free from the great bondage of desires, so difficult to avoid, are capable of liberation—no other can, even though versed in the six systems of philosophy.

8. Spirit must be sought out by intuition; liberation is not achieved by the pronunciation of the word *Brahman* without direct perception. Un-manifest spiritual consciousness begins to manifest like the dawn in the pure heart and, shining like the midday sun, illuminates the whole universe as pure awareness.

9. Deprived of the real knowledge of the Atman through great delusions, one becomes contemptible in conduct. Purity, perception of the Atman within us, cheerfulness, and concentration of mind on the self are the qualities by which a taste of eternal bliss is obtained.

10. Wise seekers must acquire discrimination between Spirit and not-Spirit in all things, as only by realizing the Self in all, which is absolute Being, can they become the bliss they seek.

11. The knowledge that Brahman and Atman are one and the same is true knowledge; with it, ignorance, although without beginning, is entirely destroyed. It can only be acquired by the perfect discrimination of Self and ego. Self is the "I" that ordains and knows. The ego seems to ordain and know but is nothing.

12. By the absence of all existence besides itself, Brahman is Truth, supreme, the only One; and when the supreme truth is realized fully, nothing remains but this.[1]

All the rest of their lessons revolve around these twelve.

Similarly all Christian doctrines swing around twelve statements from the gospels of the Christian New Testament:

1. God is Spirit, and those who worship Him must worship Him in Spirit.
2. Only One is your Father, even God. Judge not according to appearance.
3. The Father and I are One: the I am in me and you.
4. You believe in God; believe also in Me.
5. Signs shall follow those who believe.
6. I will give you a mouth and wisdom that all your adversaries shall not be able to gainsay nor resist. God doesn't measure when giving the Spirit.
7. Call no man on earth your father.
8. You are the light of the world.
9. I came not to condemn the world.
10. Heaven and earth shall eventually pass away, but My Word shall not pass away.
11. You all know where I am. The Holy Ghost shall teach you all things.
12. All things that I have heard from the Father I have told you. Your joy no one can take from you.

The principles emerging through the past century in the sciences also support these same twelve principles:

1. The universe is one interwoven *holon*,[2] the material and energetic manifestation of an underlying intelligence that is evident in the patterns of order and harmony present at all levels; all patterns

within the whole emerge out of the underlying creative intelligence; all beings are a part of that whole, and intelligence and harmony are part of our essential nature.

2. In the one whole that is the universe, there can be no separation; all the "wavicles" or "strings" that make up matter and energy are interconnected such that any action in any part of the universe acts on all of it, nonlocally, throughout space and time; I am therefore one with all things everywhere and with all that makes up all things, so my only sustainable experience is the harmony of the interconnected whole; any other experience is a dissipative structure[3] that depends on continuous flows of thought or other energy for its existence and can be dissolved easily by refocusing creative intelligence and energy on the whole or other aspects of the whole.

3. As I am one with all things everywhere and across all time, I have access to all knowledge of all beings, all emotional states, and all possible activities; my life is a pattern within the totality of these states and activities; it emerges from the particular aspect of the creative intelligence that is my imagination, and whatever I imagine becomes my experience—either effortlessly sustainable or a dissipative structure that requires continued energy for its continued existence.

4. Since I have access to all possibilities at all times, my experience is a function of what I have chosen to accept; to the extent that I choose to experience only those patterns of possibility that reflect and reinforce the harmonious whole of which I am a part, I effortlessly and enjoyably experience those; therefore, I choose to hold those patterns firmly in my mind and imagination, regardless of all appearances.

5. Because all patterns of matter and energy in the universe emerge out of creative intelligence, all my experience emerges from my particular aspect of creative intelligence, or imagination; there is no other source of experience, and to the extent that I align my imagination, thoughts, and words with the pattern of the whole, I experience harmony and the oneness of the whole.

6. The intelligence that manifests as my particular pattern of matter and energy in this holon we call the universe is capable of understanding the underlying pattern of the whole and expressing it in ways that enable me to realign any patterns across space and time; I need simply to focus my attention on the underlying and overarching pattern of harmony that lies beyond the realm of my present experience.

7. We can apply these principles with and for all other beings whom we encounter, just as we can for my own experience. We realize that all beings are a part of that whole, and intelligence and harmony are part of our essential nature.

8. We can negate that which is not an aspect of the whole for others by realizing that all experience is a dissipative structure that depends on continuous flows of thought and other energy for its existence and can be dissolved easily by refocusing energy and creative intelligence on the whole.

9. We are one with all things everywhere and across all time, with access to all knowledge of all beings, all emotional states, and all possible activities. Our individual and collective life is a pattern within the totality of these states and activities that emerges from the particular aspect of the creative intelligence that is the morphogenetic field[4] of our individuality. Knowing this, we can affirm that which truly is for others as well as ourselves.

10. Experience is a function of what we have chosen to accept; therefore, we can choose to hold those patterns firmly in mind and imagination, regardless of all appearances, in a way that leads to permanent transformation for the world and the people around us.

11. To the extent that we align imagination, thoughts, and words with the pattern of the whole, we experience the harmony of the interconnected whole, and our thoughts and words, written and spoken, contribute to the pattern of the whole through their interaction in the morphogenetic fields.

12. We can experience and express that which we call Unconditional Love throughout our whole world. We need simply to focus our

attention on the underlying and overarching pattern of harmony that lies beyond the realm of our present experience.

In these twelve principles—from whatever tradition—is outlined the esoteric philosophy of Spiritual Science. It may be summarized as in the previous example or in another way: "You have the deep glory of the One Life going on within you; so have all beings, in one constantly interconnected Whole."

Truth in these twelve statements of Spiritual Science takes our attention so entirely that the blocks are dissolved. This Science exposes this Truth and keeps it exposed in our lives and world.

When anyone exposes the glory we had with the Creator Source before the world, the whole world is transformed. Then there's nothing left on this planet that is dark and distressing or speaks of darkness or distress. As a result, the world will not rest a second in its present appearance when any one of us appears plainly here as the One we truly are now, though hidden. This is the essence of the teaching known as "the Second Coming" in both Buddhism and Christianity, "the Messiah" in Judaism, and "the Return of the Prophet" in Islam.

Once this Life is exposed or manifest in someone, that one must be Lord of all the manifest forms perceived. And this revelation occurs by thinking, writing, and speaking the words of Spiritual Science until the Spirit claims its own.

BLOCKS TO TRANSFORMATION

The gate that blocks each of us from this instant speaking aloud and boldly stepping forth as God in our glory is almost too simple and subtle for us to notice. It's any statement of criticism, any judging of ourselves or others. The various scriptures make it clear what the gates were that hid the priests and prophets. Each of the Hebrew prophets hid himself behind a gate of condemnation. Each Hindu priest hid himself behind a gate of caste. Each layman hid himself behind a gate of agreement with some prophet or priest.

The ancients' criticisms, castes, and condemnations are many. Today, our criticisms, castes, and condemnations are legion.

The profound meditations of the Hindus and Buddhists over countless years have now brought us all face-to-face with their gates of hiding. We show them plainly the gates of hiding of Western prophets, priests, and sages; the Eastern sages show us theirs. We show them the light of our gospel; they show us the light of their gospel.

They, in their language, have the same Truth we have in our language. There is only one Truth. There is only one Light, taking as many forms as the mortal mind needs to accept it. As the great Sufi poet Rumi said almost a thousand years ago, "Christian, Jew, Muslim, shaman, Zoroastrian, stone, ground, mountain, river, each has a secret way of being with the mystery, unique and not to be judged."

These gates of difference, condemnation, and judgment must disappear when we behold Truth. They're all delusions, nothing—though they seem to hide the Supreme One. They are what some call the "works of the devil," but the devil is merely the idea of lies, so a lie is all that hides the omnipresent Good.

Who shall prevent that radiant Good from working when we throw the searchlight of our own independent sun-like Self over the universe?

EMBRACING SHADOWS

Just as our body's shadow relies upon our body's activity for its movements, the Supreme Source is the substance the shadowy human ego-self relies on for its movements. Just as we know that our shadows have no life or substance of their own, so the Supreme Good knows that humanity's ego-self has no life or substance of its own, and that its ultimate happiness is the experience of being assumed into the bliss of the One.

In supreme moments, all of us have seen that there is nothing to worship, but, rather, there is something to *be*. For some people of deep faith, this experience has led to becoming mystics. For some of great intellect, it inspired the idea of being an atheist or humanist. For others, it led to the idea of shamanic revelation, ascension, or alchemy.

Isn't the highest good for anyone to be what he or she calls God? In the Book of Revelation, John tried to adore the angel, but the angel told him that angels are not greater than humanity. Both were turning their speech and thought toward the divine Truth of Life in such a way that soon they would be as celestial and alive as their Source. Both of them would soon experience the One.

Speaking Truth, Experiencing Youth

When we hear this truth, it's our business to speak it to the schools, the churches, the businesses. And we need not fear doing so! No matter what those who hear it say or do with us, we shall not be injured or die, for majesty and strength are the indestructible breath of the Supreme Presence.

The Supreme Truth is always supreme. Its ministry is to invest each of us with strength, beauty, and immortality like itself. It's the stream of eternal youth, of immortal beauty, of unchanging majesty. Nothing can defeat it. Nothing can kill it.

Truth was in the ancient past, and whoever spoke it was majestic and strong. Truth is in the living present, and whoever speaks it is majestic and strong. Truth will be the same in the future, and whoever tells it will be majestic and strong.

In the past, those who knew Truth were said to appear always as sixteen years of age. The Hindu yogi saint known as Babaji came in the early twentieth century to Paramahansa Yogananda, as well as to the explorers in Baird Spaulding's *Life and Teaching of the Masters of the Far East*, looking that age, though he had been born in the fourteenth century. The man called St. Germain is said to have appeared as youthful to those who described him in the 1700s as he had to those who described him in the 1500s.

What shall someone look like who perceives that the Truth is the Supreme and only One? Whose face, thought, speech, and action are turned to Truth alone? How do they look? What is the body formed of Truth alone? They are in our midst.

Essential Points

- There are only twelve statements in Spiritual Science, and they are present in all sacred writings and modern science.

- While there are multitudes of ways to express these twelve statements, the power of the whole twelve may be expressed in one statement: "You have the deep glory of the One Life going on within you; so have all beings, in one constantly interconnected Whole."

- The world will not rest a second in its present appearance when one of us appears plainly as the One we truly are. This revelation occurs by speaking the words of Spiritual Science until the Spirit claims its own.

- The gate that keeps each of us from instantly speaking aloud and boldly stepping forth as the One Self in our glory is any statement of criticism, any judging of ourselves or others.

- In supreme moments, all of us have seen that there is nothing to worship, but, rather, there is something to be. For some people of deep faith, this experience led to becoming mystics. For some of great intellect, it inspired the idea of being an atheist or humanist. For others, it led to shamanic revelation, ascension, or alchemy.

- The Truth in the twelve statements of Spiritual Science takes our attention so entirely that the gates barring our experience of the One disappear.

- Truth is always supreme. Nothing can defeat it. Nothing can kill it. Its ministry is to invest us with strength, beauty, and immortality like itself.

Practicing the Principle

1. Keep some of the words of Truth running in your mind continually; they reconstruct the mind along the lines of Truth, and the environment must follow. Use sticky notes, dry-erase pen on your mirrors or windows, cards in your wallet or checkbook, screensavers, phone messages—anything to help you fill your mind with these words and erode any other ideas.

2. Start a journal and write the following words at the front:
    "As Divine Mind which I am in Truth, I preach the gospel, heal the sick, cast out unhealthy passions, and raise the dead. I work the

works of Good. Divine power works through me and as me, to will and do what is my fulfillment to experience."

Each day for twenty-eight days, read these words and contemplate them for at least half an hour, writing your responses to them in your journal. Highlight every time that one of these statements is fulfilled in your life. As you study these words, make them your own.

LESSON 6
UNDERSTANDING

In the early sixteenth century, Paracelsus[1] told his neighbors that if they wished to awaken their inherent magical powers, they should continually read John's Book of Revelation at the end of the New Testament. The "magical powers" he was talking about are the hidden faculties that all human beings possess. Almost two thousand years earlier, the Chinese philosopher Confucius[2] said that if anyone would stimulate these faculties, they would not need to study books; they would experience an understanding of the books' essence that was superior to the mind that wrote them.

The Book of Revelation is written in figurative language that describes the experience of the great judgment and understanding present in the One Mind and therefore in all minds everywhere. Paracelsus understood that when we internalize this, all the powers of mind are ours, and we use them skillfully.

There's a similar practice of directing the mind toward bodily conditions and bringing out their health and beauty. This was the first claim made by Mary Baker Eddy's book *Science and Health with Key to the Scriptures*, based on the work of her teacher, Phineas Parkhurst Quimby, in the 1860s.[3] It's the essence of Louise Hay's *You Can Heal Your Life*, written a hundred years later.

There's a practice of directing special attention toward the internal vision and causing the eyes to see plainly. This is developed in the many vision, visualization, and eye-improvement exercises available today.

There's a practice of attending strictly to mental understanding and drawing aside the ideas that obscure our wisdom. The lessons described here and my other books are intended to accomplish this result.

There's a practice for becoming one with the Good we have sought. To become one with the Good in a situation and so transform it is to "treat" that situation. When Eddy wrote *Science and Health*, she described most clearly the principle of treatment, saying that whenever we commune with anybody or anything in any way or fashion, we "treat" with them. We may or may not mean to do so, but the result is the same. And Eddy is said to have unintentionally treated the people around her often in her later years, having treated thousands of people intentionally over decades.

There's one Presence that we cannot elude or be absent from: the omnipresence of Supreme Wisdom. The more you understand a subject, the clearer that subject will be for the people around you. Your knowledge is a "treatment" they receive. As an example, the Greek statesman Aristides[4] told Socrates that wisdom penetrated him whenever Socrates approached him and that it felt like the wisdom of Socrates.

Distinguishing Individual Mind from Divine Mind

When speakers talk about the mind as an instrument, they are quoting from the doctrine of the Hindu priests on the mortal, human mind. They do not mean the Great Presence whose name is Immortal, Divine Understanding, and Intelligence.

That's not an instrument. It doesn't do anything for us. It doesn't even speak our language, yet when we look toward it, we speak a language. It doesn't think anything, yet when we look toward it, we think thoughts. The Hindu texts called the Upanishads say, "That which cannot be expressed in words but through which all expression comes, this I know to be Brahman. That which cannot be thought by the mind but by which all thinking comes, this I know is Brahman. That which cannot be seen but by which the eye sees, know that to be Brahman."[5]

Many New Thought speakers and writers say, "There is one Mind thinking thoughts. It's the only Mind: Divine, Immortal Wisdom." They're referring to this great Presence whose influence on our mind is so powerful when we look toward it that we think like the Creator.

Then again, these speakers and writers use the term ego for both the human aspect that governs our bodies and the Divine Ego, who knows nothing of the body, yet when we look toward it, our body takes on a new radiance.

Some speakers and writers talk mostly of nature and intellect. Examine them closely and you'll perceive they are describing the unreal, illusionary phenomena of the physically tangible world of matter. It's an interesting system, but it is not Spirit. It's what Eddy called the dream creation. It's what the Buddhists call maya, which means "changeable" and is therefore not the Unchanging Reality but delusion.

Spiritual Science recommends fixing the mind on the Eternal One. Krishna said, "With mind and intellect fixed in Me, thou shalt doubtless come to Me alone."[6] The Nazarene said it this way, "Seek first the kingdom of God, and all these things will be added unto you."[7]

You must have what the Theosophists call discriminative knowledge to separate promptly and without error the ego-self human mind from the divine. You must separate, promptly and without error, the human mortal mind from the divine Immortal Mind. You must separate any perceivable material formulation from the spiritually visible Spirit.

In the same way, it's our business to distinguish instantly between the concentration of our minds on one universal Spirit equally present everywhere and the concentration of our minds on the changing moon or even a word.

For example, would you say there were two boats because you saw a reflection of your boat in the water? If I speak of one, can't you tell instantly whether I speak of the unreal boat that glides beneath your real boat or of the boat you are sailing in? If I speak of the mind as an instrument, don't you know instantly whether I am speaking of what glides along dealing with material things or of that One Intelligence from whose storehouse we draw an understanding of how to handle the mind we use? If I speak of one, aren't you instantly aware whether I'm speaking of the Eternal One or of an inverted image?

Further, though one teacher may talk of mind as if there were two minds, a human mind and a Divine Mind, will you think there are two minds? Is there any separate human spirit in reality? Is there any mortal or deluded mind in reality? Is there any individual human or carnal mind in reality?

Focus and Become

When the human, or mortal, mind thinks about Immortal Mind, the Immortal Mind shines on it and through it. If we look toward this Presence continually, we begin to look like it. The mind looks at the Presence and shines till every part and particle of the body are transfigured.

Suppose you think that the substance of an antibiotic is God. If so, the power of God will stand out from it, and it will have a healing effect. God, as our Good, is Health whenever spoken of in any way, anywhere.

Suppose you come to know that the substance of your voice, the substance of your glance, the substance of your touch is God. Then the power of God will be exposed in the same way by your saying so. Everything you do will have a healing quality, based on what you've said, believing it to be so.

Look and Speak

The very mention of the Omnipotent One is the mention of a healing power. One name of God is Allah. Another is Krishna. Another, Jesus Christ. Another is the Great Spirit. Another, Om. It's a wonderful discloser of hidden faculties to look toward the Great Spirit in all things. The greatest miracles are wrought by looking toward the Great Presence of Wisdom.

No matter what errors you keep in your mind, you can be a miracle worker if you look only toward this mighty Presence. You may even believe that there is a devil, like the great German faith healer Johann Joseph Gassner, who cured all kinds of disease by applying the name Jesus Christ to men and women as a present, irresistible health. You may imagine God as a great and glorious male figure sitting on a throne as the faith-cure workers of some Christian sects do, and like them, cure all manner of disease by applying the name Christ or Jesus Christ to the people as a present, irresistible power for health. Errors of mortal mind count nothing, simply nothing, while you are looking so steadily toward this almighty Presence before you. As Krishna tells us in the Bhagavad Gita, "Even if the most sinful worships Me, with devotion to none else, he too should indeed be regarded as righteous, for he has rightly resolved."[8]

ALL THAT REMAINS

We can be free to the flow of an unprejudiced idea through us by keeping our mind facing the Divine Mind until the divine is all there is of us. Maya, the mother of Siddhartha Gautama, did so, seeing and hearing only the unimaginable Beauty that called her, and gave birth to the Awakened One. Mary, the mother of Jesus, did so, gave Wisdom free passage through her mind, and brought forth a Wonderful Counselor by being entirely divine in her thought.

We can sit in the silence, study sacred texts, or perform sacred rituals to experience that flow, but the best way we have for looking toward this Presence is talking to it. We're focusing our attention on whomever we speak to. The Hebrew prophet Hosea said, "Let us take with us words and go unto our God."[9] The whole of the Bhagavad Gita is a conversation between a seeker and his Lord.

This is because there's an instant after speaking when we do not speak. There's an instant after thinking when we do not think. This instant is what Deepak Chopra calls "the gap" in his many books and lectures. It's the silence in heaven John speaks of in Revelation. Maya felt it at the moments of the Buddha's conception and birth, and Mary felt it at the moment she conceived the Christ.

We may bring forth our own ordained works by being so lost in the sight of this Presence that we are That only. This is the essence of Eastern mind-emptying meditations and also of Unity founder Charles Fillmore's instruction to sit, "waiting and listening" for some time each day.[10]

An Arab legend taught the drawing power of the One in the story of a mountain that, when a ship sailed in sight of it, would cause the craft to go all to pieces. The nails, the steel bands, the iron chains, and the metal fastenings and tools would leave the ship and fly to the mountain. Then the wood, hay, and stubble of the ship would disappear into the deep.

To apply the metaphor, if we sail the ship of our mind toward the mountain of God here at our center by thinking and thinking of only that Eternal One, all that has held our mortal ego-self shall be pulled away and we shall no more be human beings but transcendent, divine beings. We'll be what the genuine quality, the true Substance of us, already is: divinity manifest. The mortal mind, which we have called an instrument, will be like the wood, hay, stubble—pure nothingness. The Divine Mind will be all there is of us.

In that moment, the flesh as a changing, homely, hateful yet loveable thing will be gone. The mind, with its errors, with its strife to be true, will be gone. Only the eternal body in its beauty, only the Divine Mind with its brilliant understanding will be left.

THE POWER OF UNDERSTANDING

Understanding is the wellspring of life.

In Eddy's *Science and Health*, which introduced Christian Science as a healing method, we find the idea that understanding is the divine Self at work. That is, if one sits in the presence of a sick person and understands that their disease is nothing, delusion, and understands that the person is divinely whole and perfect, that person is sure to get well at once. Their divine spiritual nature comes forward, and they show good health. This method has been learned by many over the past 150 years and its effects documented thousands of times within both Christian Science and the New Thought movement.

On this same principle, even severely retarded children have brilliant minds at the center of their being, and if any of us understands this to be true, the intelligence of that child will come forward in proportion to our understanding. This is made beautifully evident in the film *The Boys Next Door*, a story of the love and wisdom expressed by the residents of a care facility for the mentally handicapped.

We learn a habit of concentrating our own capacity for understanding toward one thing or another according to what science we are studying. If we're studying the body, we use expensive equipment and elaborate experiments to discover and understand the internal activities of the body as it takes in, releases, and becomes energy. If we're studying the yoga sutras, we focus our attention on any material thing to find the central intelligence of that thing to expose all relevant information. For instance, we are told to concentrate our mind upon the moon to know all about the fixed stars.

The Buddhists and Hindus both teach that to concentrate the mind upon any word brings more of it into our lives. For example, focusing our attention on the word *friendship* will draw friends to us as to magnets.[11]

"Come, let us reason together," said the Lord to the prophet Isaiah.[11] Understanding is One. It is all in all to humanity as the sun is the all in all of the earth's atmosphere. Focused on the appearance of lack, our own divine Understanding burns it off just as the focus of the sun's rays on any object burns it off.

Concentrating the sun's rays through the magnifying glass, we burn wood, hay, stubble. Concentrating all our understanding into our Emmanuel Name, we burn away sorrow and foolishness, matter and mind.

To understand is to be wise in our belief and unbelief. So let us attend to our own understanding, our own sunshine, our own True Nature. Shall not we be the Good that sets the unhappy world moving into peace? By understanding our own splendor, we burn down the barriers that stop our ears from hearing the wonderful choirs now singing near us. By understanding our own bright splendor of Intelligence, we burn off the blinders—the prejudices and assumptions—that hide the sight of what is truly going on around us.

FULFILLMENT

Do you realize that there is one topic on which you can focus your understanding that will erase your own ego-self human mind and show only the Divine Mind?

Whatever we seek diligently to understand, there comes a moment when Understanding springs forth in some particular direction. One person seeks to understand health and searches and studies until the thought of Health fills the mind. In that moment, the seeker's understanding of Health radiates like the rays of the sun and heals all manner of disease wherever they are.

One person lets a streak of bright sunshine go free by much thought of and about Spirit. At that moment, wherever they walk they speak brilliantly, originally, powerfully of the Good, and we wonder at them.

Others let their sunshine of Understanding stream through them toward the world by focusing their thoughts till they burn through all that is unhappiness. Everyone is happy when they think about such people.

We all can work miracles with that same line of reasoning.

Do you know why we speak these wonderful and almost unbelievable things to a world that has all its attention turned toward matter? It's because mind pulls matter around with it. As experiments in physics and biology both have shown, the material world follows the mental.

Won't you love to see the prophecies of the good and noble of all ages fulfilled, when, by our understanding, we've straightened up all who are downcast and beautified all imperfect things? This fulfillment is promised to be the first indication that the understanding fire within us has been focused on the One whose name is Understanding.

FOCUS

Do you realize that we must speak of understanding if we are to understand? Whatever we focus our mind on, write about, and speak about, we understand and become. No more; no less.

If you want to see the fine stream of light that streams between the small air molecules around us, you must watch for it and think about it constantly.

Do you know what you can focus your grieved soul on until that part of you that is capable of grieving is lost and the Self that is above all human passions and distress is your own experience? Of course, as we have seen, it must be that Self that you wish to experience.

Consider:

We, by thinking of God, by whatever name, understand All. Thinking of what we call God we are thinking of a fire that will consume everything except itself; therefore, as our walls feed the flames, we're all illuminated, inspired in some way.

Thinking and thinking of the Immortal mind we call God, we understand the Intelligence who speaks as humans or other forms of being everywhere.

Thinking and still thinking of God, we feel the fires burning down other gates and barriers, and we work other miracles. Thinking and thinking more of God, we burn down still other bars, still more plastering; we work other miracles.

Thinking and thinking of God still more, we find ourselves God. We do all things. The former heaven and earth are no longer visible to us. As God is the light, we are the light of our world. We are the heat of our world as God is the heat of the universe.

Thinking and thinking of God melts the rocks and the mountains.

> **Thinking and thinking of God dissolves flesh and the glorious body that was with us before the world was, that is with us now and we can never be separate from, becomes visible.***

Spend some time with what you have just read. How much divine Intelligence has shed Itself through you now?

We are not changing, discordant creatures. We do not have to walk among sorrowful beings. Do you see upright, irresistible men, women, and animals? Are they out of the reach of pain or hunger in your eyes? Does everyone look handsome, healthy, and brilliant with wisdom in your eyes? That is the truth that sets us free.

THE ETERNAL NAME

We understand the Eternal by feeding the mind on a Name of that Eternal.

How long have you been making your own particular name of God, your Emmanuel Name, the one theme on which you have fed your mind? Do you eat the Eternal Name with your mind as you eat your breakfast with your body? Do you eat the Name with your mind as you eat your dinner? Is your God all in all to you? Through and through you? This is what's meant by Practicing the Presence, bringing one's awareness of the divine into all aspects of one's life and activity to the point where the divine is and truly felt as one's all in all.

The Emmanuel Name stands for one who dwells at the center and moves Life and Spirit through the universe or who does nothing with life and Spirit, according to choice. When we turn our mind toward that Name, we arrive at the same freedom. All have the Emmanuel freedom at their center.

Whether we know that Name as Brahman, Beloved, Isis, Inanna, Krishna, Rama, Mithra, or Jesus Christ, it is One Emmanuel.

---

*Hopkins's words slightly edited for readability. For the original quote, see page 184.

If we understand the One through concentration of mind upon the Emmanuel name, we do not believe in the reality of matter; we understand that what appears to be matter is energy formed by our consciousness. We do not believe that evil or sickness can conquer; we understand that there is only one power in all that is, and that power is for harmony, balance, and order. We believe that the spirit of humanity will rise in unconquerable majesty if we see it in people. We believe their spirit will rise in them and be noble, healthy, beautiful. We see it in all humanity everywhere; therefore, we believe in it and testify that we do see. And our testimony is true.

The Emmanuel conquers by conscious knowledge of all beings' Spiritual origin and everlasting quality and makes the earth a plaything. The Emmanuel handles serpents as the master of serpents, through conscious acquaintance with the One Source of All. The Emmanuel calls health into sight and life into sight through making health and life as obedient as serpents. By our conscious knowledge of the Source of Life, the Emmanuel presence will fire all of us with understanding of how to experience life, health, strength, and peace in all the world.

POWER IN THE NAME

When I understand the Emmanuel Name through meditating upon the Om as the Hindu and Buddhist yogis do, or through walking the path of the Beauty Way, or by choosing to let the Christ into my heart, I become Emmanuel in the divine Name that no human tongue speaks, that no one knows who sees anything that hurts or discourages. And so shall you.

Whoever understands the Infinite One through concentrating upon the Emmanuel Name has the power of the Holy Spirit. Whoever understands Eternity through concentrating all the attention of their mind upon the Emmanuel Name remembers all they knew with the Creator in the beginning and can tell boldly and brilliantly all that they have always known. This is the way of the Tao. It's also the way of those who've learned to "read," or access and see, the Akashic records, the repository of mystic knowledge collected from the cosmos.

In the Corpus Hermeticum it's said that the one Nöus (the Source Consciousness, given the name Pymander) said, "These things, O Asclepius, will appear to be true if you understand them; but if you understand them not, incredible. For to understand is to believe; but not to believe is not to understand."[12]

The Emmanuel Name rushes from our center to the circumference of all things now. We realize we need no longer hold on to the Name; we are the Name. We seek no more of God; we accept that we are the same Substance and Mind. We speak no longer of the loving presence we've called Emmanuel; we are Emmanuel. We're not seeking to understand; we are the understanding. We're not in the world or of the world; we are all that is. We're no longer merely human; we are the divinity that is in all, working through all for the good of all.

To know yourself is understanding. I understand my Self; therefore, I understand all there is to understand. And when I realize that I am one in being with all, then everyone in all in my world understands with me.

Essential Points

- The Book of Revelation is written in figurative language that describes the experience of the great judgment and understanding present in the One Mind and therefore in all minds everywhere. When we internalize this, all the powers of mind are ours. We use them skillfully.
- A treatment is a method for transforming a situation, and whenever we commune with anybody or anything in any way or fashion, we treat them.
- No matter what errors you keep in your mind, you can be a miracle worker if you look fully toward the mighty Presence of Immortal Mind.
- The best way we have for looking toward this Presence is talking to it. We're focusing our attention on whomever we speak to.
- There's an instant after speaking when we do not speak. There's an instant after thinking when we do not think. This instant is the silence in heaven spoken of in scriptures.

- Thinking of only the Eternal One, we shall no longer be human beings but transcendent, divine beings. We shall be what the genuine quality, the true substance of us, already is—divinity manifest.

- Whoever understands the Infinite One through concentrating upon the Emmanuel Name has the power of the Holy Spirit. Whoever understands Eternity through concentrating all the attention of their mind upon the Emmanuel Name remembers all they knew with the Creator in the beginning and can tell boldly and brilliantly all that they have always known.

- To know yourself is understanding. I understand my Self; therefore, I understand all there is to understand. And when I realize that I am one in being with all, then everyone in all in my world understands with me.

Practicing the Principle

Once a week (Saturday, being the sixth day of the week, is best) take an idea from this Science and reason with it until the light of understanding breaks over and through you, thrilling your body with a cool fire of recognition. Breathe in the Spirit of Understanding so you are prepared to meet the world with your own free independence of thought, able to make nothing of its worst appearances and go forward in harmony, balance, and delight.

LESSON 7
WORKS OF TRUTH

A fter the ego-mind and its perceptions are dissolved from the claim of being an instrument of thought, our awareness is expanded into the knowledge of being the Source Itself. Then the whole world, with all its people and all things above, beneath, and around it, is exposed in its actuality. Nothing has been changed, but the Truth of all has been revealed.

RECEPTIVITY

Every day we experience something addressing the heart that the eyes cannot see, just as something addresses the ears that the hands cannot touch. Each of these conversations, though they seem to be normal human interaction, is an indicator of the one divine speech that's going on all the time. And we must be open to receive it.

Perfect stillness is entire openness. Entire openness is the reception of the All-Knowledge. The command to the Hebrews, "Be still and know that I am,"[1] is the language of the Knowing Mind which our thinking mind symbolizes. Stillness makes our sense organs, with all their peculiar ways of speaking, open receivers for the in-pouring of the Absolute and the resulting transformation of our ego-self, thinking mind.

On a much smaller scale, we see this principle at work when we use a voice-activated phone or speakerphone. The receiver can't take in what the other person is saying unless the line is silent. Then the receiver can take in everything.

The same applies to character readers or psychics: their minds become receptive for you to imprint your character on them. If they were entirely open to you, their being would be lost in your being and your will, as trance mediums are to the entities that inhabit them.

This is how we become entirely lost in the Absolute—and this is what the apostle Paul called our "reasonable service," suggesting that when we are entirely open, we are in service. "Not my will, but Thine, be done," said Jesus the Nazarene.[2] When we lose our ego-sense of self in the Absolute, we let our mortal will be replaced by the divine Will, and so our fulfillment is assured. "With their minds and lives entirely absorbed in Me, enlightening each other and always speaking of Me, they are satisfied and delighted," said Krishna.[3] This is the communion with the divine that is the desired end of all mystical paths.

You can see that no one would be as powerful as those who have been totally receptive to the Absolute Power. This receptivity is called meekness in the New Testament, and it becomes Omnipotence when fulfilled. The Nazarene demonstrated the process in his life: "I am meek and lowly of heart," Jesus said early on.[4] "I have overcome the world" is the message at the tomb.[5] "All power is given unto me in heaven and in earth" are some of the last words the disciples heard.[6] This is the progression he taught by example.

Bringing Forth

In the seventh statement of Genesis, Moses said that the earth, which is a symbol for mind, would bring forth works. "Let the earth bring forth."[7] This means that mind becomes brilliant with understanding through meekness and so serves the Good it has sought.

The mind, once receptive, serves by "bringing forth," and it brings forth in many ways. Water is receptive to its thought or spoken word, as

Masaru Emoto demonstrated with his crystal formations in Japan,[8] and it changes into wine, as it did for the Nazarene at Cana,[9] or into whatever substance you please.

The Emmanuel Mind is wide awake, wide-open consciousness. It performs no miracles accidentally. It's as thoroughly competent to do the next miracle presented as the first one. As *A Course in Miracles* notes on the first page, "There is no order of difficulty in miracles."

So why don't Christians who profess receptivity to their Father work every miracle with prompt and equal skill? They do not because they're not conscious of their Emmanuel Selves. Any miracles they experience are not the work of understanding but of a momentary openness. Unlike advanced yogis, called swamis and gurus in the Hindu tradition, they have not trained their minds to be completely receptive. Unlike the shamans of indigenous cultures, they have believed themselves to be separated from their Good.

Conscious miracle working is consciousness of omnipresent Omnipotence.

In truth, there's no need for miracles in the estimation of one who has so let go that they experience no mind, no life, no thought, no language. Instead, they let whatever is remain as it truly Is. Like Eckhart Tolle in the first days of his awakening,[10] they see only beauty, only light, and experience only love, only peace, only well-being.

They see Spirit manifesting in the tree and see not a tree but a light-filled expression of the divine. They see the Spirit expressing in the convict rather than a convict, and when that Truth is mentioned, It is exposed to others. This is bringing forth.

When an event that's not limited by time is mentioned, its timelessness is exposed. This is bringing forth.

When the Being that has never heard of death or life is mentioned, It is exposed. This is bringing forth.

When the Heart that has never heard of mind is mentioned, It is exposed. This is bringing forth.

The heart's language is spoken by the tongue. The ears' language is spoken by the tongue. Life's language is spoken by the tongue. Death's language is reported by the tongue. Therefore, the wise Hebrew king Solomon said, "Death and life are in the power of the tongue." And again, he said, "The tongue of the wise is health."[11]

Likewise, the language of the being that never thinks of life or death is spoken by the tongue. The language of what is absolutely changeless is spoken by the tongue, and whatever is unalterable Truth must stand forth. This is bringing forth. The nearer the tongue comes to telling the unalterable Truth, the more perfect is the bringing forth of health, life, and intelligence in ourselves and in our world.

Essential Stillness

While someone describes wonderful music perfectly, we see neither the music nor the reporter; eyesight is forgotten. Likewise, the ears are deaf while we gaze upon a wonderful painting or awesome sunset. So all the senses, as well as mind and thought, are still when the tongue skillfully speaks the language of the divine Truth that always is. "Eye hath not seen, nor ear heard, neither hath it entered into the heart of one to conceive what God hath prepared for them that love Him."[12] When we speak the language of Omnipresence, the mind extends itself to greatness.

A sage of India once showed a German traveler some old books at the traveler's request. While doing so, however, the sage told him that true sages never write books, never speak, and never make an effort to teach. They had stilled their mind by silencing all its operations to receive the imprint of the ever-present Wisdom, and whoever should come into their presence would receive what they knew in like manner or remain ignorant.

Dissolving into Oneness

The spark in our center is the Omnipresence of the One. It's exposed for each of us by some clash in our experience—an illness, a divorce, an economic downturn—and our world dissolves. All the structures and formulations built on our old patterns of thought and feeling come unglued, and it seems that nothing remains. It's like when a spark is ignited in the world; houses are burned and people are left with nothing in the material. Then in the throes of the calamity, each one finds a deeper strength, showing themselves to be, at their core, the same substance as the spark. Similarly, the whole human mind, experiencing all its familiar thoughts and friendly senses burned away, finds a new way of being and is seen to be the spark of that Absolute that stays and waits. They become totally receptive and open.

Theosophists say that in the raja yoga philosophy of India, the earth ego and the Divine Ego are shrouded by five sheaths that the right understanding will dissolve.[13] The right understanding they refer to is the true statement of what divinity is, what nature is, what humanity is, what life is. The "I" that is aware of the body and is hurt or pleased by what happens to the body is the human ego-self. This "I" is one of the sheaths covering the divine Spark. By dissolving the thoughts and feelings of the human "I" or ego-self, the shining Absolute breaks forth and the gross body disappears.

In a book of translated aphorisms by Tukaram Tatya, we read, "A wise man must acquire the discrimination of Spirit and not-Spirit, as only by realizing the Self which is Absolute being, consciousness, and bliss, he himself becomes bliss."[14] Dissolving our old world, our old sense of self, we become aware of the bliss that is our true nature.

All the points of Spiritual Science are directed to the dissolving of the ego's sheaths, to reveal the Divine Spark, the Higher Self. It does this first by understanding the soul, mind, nature, and matter; second by understanding Ego, God, Brahman, the invisible, unnameable One; and third by ceasing from understanding altogether.

Never till the tongue is speechless, the mind dissolved, the ego-self melted can Truth be known, be exposed. Then all doctrine, all understanding is seen not to *be* at all. Then the "I," the Ego, the so-called God, is seen not to be. Then even Truth Absolute, as we describe it, is seen not to be.

The Taoists remind us, "That which Is the Way is not that which can be told."

There is something that is free from all union: that which *Is*. That which is free of all limitations is divine. Hence those who look toward freedom by this Science are looking toward the divine One.

To look toward freedom by understanding is to use an instrument to view the heavens or the insects of the earth. Understanding deals with unimaginable infinity through telescopic information. Understanding deals with the inconceivably small through microscopic information. Each takes the mind from its habitual tracks and shows new territories to the senses.

But no understanding is Truth. The Truth is unknowable by that which is dissolvable. Truth is known only to itself. All explanation is but an instrument to distract the mind's native knowledge from Truth. The Emmanuel purpose is to set the mind free from doctrine and explanation, to turn it to see the Absolute, and thus, to be the Absolute.

Ultimately, all science teaches us to ignore science. As the master craftsman drops the rules and standards that had been imposed by the teacher during apprenticeship, so Understanding leads to dropping the ego-self's understanding; talk of divinity leads to no talk of divinity; the scientist becomes the mystic. Likewise, Spiritual Science dissolves understanding. Having brought forth a heavenly world, it dissolves itself into bliss. Its only mission is finished when we know there is nothing to say, for there is nothing to know.

Only a firm mind brings forth a world. Only what we call God brings forth what IS.

Essential Points

- Something addresses the heart that the eyes cannot see, just as something addresses the ears that the hands cannot touch. And each of these conversations is an indicator of the one divine speech that's going on all the time.
- No one could be as powerful as those who have been totally receptive to the speech of the Absolute. This receptivity is the Emmanuel Mind. It's called meekness in the New Testament, and it becomes Omnipotence when fulfilled.

- The Emmanuel Mind is wide-open consciousness, Pure Awareness.
- Why don't Christians who profess receptivity to their Father work every miracle with prompt and equal skill? They are not conscious of their Emmanuel selves.
- Conscious miracle working is consciousness of Omnipresent Omnipotence. In truth, for anyone who has so let go of ego-self that they experience no mind, no life, no thought, no language, no miracles *need* to be brought about. Instead, they let whatever is remain as it truly Is.
- The spark in our center is the Omnipresence of the One. For each of us, by some clash in our experience—an illness, a divorce, an economic downturn—it is exposed, and our world dissolves. The "I" that is aware of the body and is hurt or pleased by what happens is the human ego. By dissolving the human "I," or ego, the shining Absolute breaks forth.
- All the points of Spiritual Science are directed to dissolving the ego and revealing the Divine Spark, the Higher Self. It does this first by understanding the soul, mind, nature, and matter; second, by understanding Ego, God, Brahman, the invisible unnameable One; third, by ceasing from understanding altogether.
- Ultimately, all sciences teach us to ignore science. As the master drops the rules learned in apprenticeship, so Understanding leads to dropping the ego-self's understanding.
- Spiritual Science dissolves itself. Its only mission is finished when we know there is nothing to say, for there is nothing to know. Truth is known only to itself.

Practicing the Principle

1. Take half an hour each morning for simply being still and receptive. Be open to receiving some special message of Truth for yourself that you can focus on for the day. Set aside another half hour early in the afternoon to listen for some words of Truth in the world.
2. Throughout the day, practice speaking and thinking only praiseful thoughts toward your Free Self and that of your neighbor. Every

time you see your neighbor apparently sick or poor or unhappy, remember their real Self, the Good that they are in Truth.

3. Remember that "where two or more are gathered," the Presence is always felt. Be open to the possibility of including a friend or partner in your praise and work,[15] someone to face you with your own Divine Self when you may have forgotten it. Set aside some time each week to check in and support each other in guided meditation or prayer—for yourselves, for others you know, for the world.

LESSON 8
SPIRITUAL LIGHT

There are three interpretations given to the scriptures of the world:

1. Literal—accepting what the words describe as existing in material experience;
2. Mental—accepting what the words describe as metaphors or symbols for a mental or emotional experience;
3. Spiritual—accepting what the words describe as always an aspect of the One.

Take the words "bottomless pit" as an example. Literalists see and feel according to common sense that there must be a bottomless hole to contain all the billions of inhabitants of the universe who have erred and stepped off the path (which is what the word *trespasses* in the most common Christian prayer refers to). This is the focus of fundamentalist Muslims and Christians alike.

Those who interpret the scriptures from a mental perspective declare that the only bottomless pit is the desire of the mind. Nothing, they explain, can satisfy human desire. Desire is a bottomless vacuum: give people everything they ask for and they are still ready to suck in something else. This is the focus of Buddhists and Hindu yogis.

Those who take the world's scriptures spiritually are found declaring that One—called God, the Absolute, Good, Brahman, Allah, and infinite other Names—absorbs all who have being and existence. The unlimited One is the consuming fire that swallows death and hell, heaven and paradise, being and not being. Is it not written that death and hell are swallowed up in victory? Is it not written that Emmanuel, whether it be the state of being called Christ in the New Testament or the state of being called *sat-chit-ananda* in the Hindu scriptures, is the victory that swallows death and hell?

The New Testament describes God consuming the universe. "I draw all men unto Me"[1]; "All things are delivered unto Me of the Father."[2] Who else is so glorious in peace as the One who consumes and contains all things and is satisfied? It's the Higher Self of each of us that calls for all things to be consumed in our being. It's God containing God; Brahman containing Atman, Self containing self.

This understanding is illumination, the shining light. This is smokeless fire. This is the light of the world.

ILLUMINATING YOUR PATH

Whatever interpretation of scripture pleases you best is your illumination. And your illumination is your doctrine. Doctrine acts as a light to the feet and a lamp shining on the pathway. It can be one's defense and gloriousness or their Hades and pain.

The Hebrew scriptures tell us, "My word," saith the Lord, "is a lamp unto your feet."[3] Your proclamation of what is, according to your interpretation, will be sent on ahead of you, and you will find every stone and tree moving itself either out of your way to give you free transit or into your way to hinder you.

"The letter kills," says a bold text in the New Testament.[4] That is, whoever takes the scripture as it reads literally must live by material laws and go out as matter goes out, namely, in death. For we find that the literal interpretation of the Bible, Qur'an, and other scriptures preaches a doctrine of death.

That interpretation also leads to torment and distress. Those who take the lake of fire to be a literal, material Hades must feel greatly the heat of strife and turmoil in their life, for their errors have a double torment, as both their mind and body enter into daily tribulation.

Experiences are also open to interpretation. For example, blindness is a function of the reader's interpretation. All the blindness there is must be mental blindness, since mental states are reflected as shadows in the world and make bodily states.

Likewise with deafness. To say that you cannot hear the voice of the Lord will not only shut your mind to the knowledge of God but will also affect your outer ears. Very likely, you'll have a number of deaf people making your pathway more difficult daily. And because mental states formulate the body, unless you let the idea go, you soon may not be able to hear well yourself.

But if you believe that the One containing all things can't hear anything outside itself, you will hear only that voice. Such a doctrine turns you toward yourself. It's your own word lighting your own mind.

So you see that you may experience some deaf people or may yourself have physical deafness if you please. You may also have a world of people hearing what pleases them while being deaf to what does not please them through the doctrine you hold. They may hear what is not pleasing to them if you hold either the interpretations of matter or mind while you read the sacred scriptures of the world—and what is most pleasing if you hold the spiritual interpretation.

Your doctrine is a lamp that lights your life with splendor or with a lurid haze.

The literal interpretation, the letter of the world's sacred scriptures can make you believe that all is darkness in the world and over the world. The letter of scripture would have you think you don't have the light of understanding but must get the light from God.

The mental interpretation of the world's scriptures can make you think that you must speak and think in order to have power and bring forth good. It leads to the formation of declarations, affirmations, and denials.

The spiritual understanding or the God-interpretation would show you that all you have to do is be. All you have to think is nothing. All you have to speak is nothing.

Only the spiritual interpretation can illuminate your life with what satisfies you. By this lamp, you can find every object and every event a subdued instrument for your use without effort on your part. Your only effort is carrying your doctrine as people carry a candle.

THE ROLE OF DOCTRINE

Our doctrine is the set of beliefs we think and feel about who we are and how the universe works. Our minds are subject to our doctrine. The things around us are subject to our doctrine. And things and mind are exposed by the doctrine we hold.

Why do people dig in the gold mines or work greedily to get their gold? Because the doctrine they believe in compels their efforts in one of these directions.

Could they have a doctrine that would undo effort? They could. This doctrine of Spiritual Science undoes effort for all minds. In the midst of a world of effort, people with this doctrine lie down or sit still while all things arrange themselves in order to please them. As the Hebrew scriptures read, the Lord "makes me lie down in green pastures."[5] And in the Christian: "Take no thought."[6]

This doctrine of the Spiritual Science is the doctrine of ease. It's the doctrine that reveals things that are already formed, based on the oldest teaching of humanity. Things are already created before they appear in our experience. Those who hold this doctrine have a lamp that exposes what is already made. Therefore, the only thing we need to obtain is spiritual doctrine.

The doctrines we hold are the light on our path, and whatever that path may be, it must lead us ultimately to the One. So if another holds a different doctrine, do not disturb them. Do not despise them. Their doctrine is the most powerful thing in their world. Let each one try their own lamp and see what is already made from the light their own doctrine throws upon it.

Mohammed gave up the opinions of others when he received his revelation. The Nazarene received no doctrines from others. In this Science we learn that turning toward our deeper understanding is the only repenting that the Eternal One knows anything about. If my doctrine turns me toward the flame that cannot be extinguished, that will burn forever within my own being, I have repented; I've turned toward the One. By so doing, I no longer look to another for my information, my inspiration, my happiness. Instead, I find all this in the Highest Good, the One Self of all.

The Bhagavad Gita tells us that those who focus on Krishna as embodiment of Om "are satisfied and delighted."[7] In the Hebrew scripture, Elisha's lamp exposed the horsemen and chariots no army of men could fight against. Persistently holding that lamp, Elisha's servant's eyes also beheld the celestial warriors.[8] The New Testament doctrine of Jesus promises that every eye shall see and every tongue confess all that is exposed by the steady holding of the Nazarene's candle toward the presence of Heaven.[9]

DECREE AND LET BE

Following the literal interpretation of the scriptures, your doctrine shines on what is already done and sees nothing but a mass of matter. It is crude but waiting for you to use it to manufacture something wonderful.

Following the mental interpretation your doctrine shines on the kingdom and shows you a mass of matter and mind that is crude but yielding to your orders. You read, "You shall decree a thing and it shall be established unto thee,"[10] so you decree. Understanding this, someone steadily holding their own lamp of abundant provision in a city full of people who appear to be starving can cause the abundant provisions to be revealed to the populace while not stirring from his or her chair.

If you understand the doctrine of "I decree" but your former doctrine said that difficult, hard labor was the lot and law of life, you may still find yourself struggling. Your world has not yet come unglued, and your new doctrine of decree is not yet your heartfelt doctrine. The lamp of labor still sheds its lurid haze on the kingdom of Absolute Perfection, and your decree takes time and mental effort to come into your experience.

Decree shines its beams on the divine kingdom at your hand, however you interpret it. The "I decree" doctrine is powerful in bringing forth what you seek, but is not yet revealing what Is. At this point all is ease but is yet artificial, unsatisfactory.

Then as you move forward in this Science, the realization comes that there is nothing to be created—all that we ever could need or desire is created, is at hand. There is nothing to be done—all is done. Therefore, the doctrine of "let be" is the one doctrine that sheds the perfect light on the Kingdom of God here in the broad daylight of our deeper understanding.

That which was and is and ever will be cannot be altered by any doctrine anyone may preach, but the doctrine of the Absolute will cause what Is now to show itself—not as what is desirable but as that which Is: heavenly peace, Nirvana, Samadhi, Paradise. This is the doctrine our Self had before the doctrines of humanity invited us to see the Kingdom from other standpoints. This is the light we had then and are forever.

THE HEART

The heart is our link with All That Is. It contains the One.

"I am seated in the hearts of all; from Me are memory, knowledge," said Krishna in the Bhagavad Gita.[11] "I, dwelling within their Self, destroy the darkness born of ignorance by the luminous lamp of knowledge."[12]

The Sufi sage Rumi told us, "We may know who we are or we may not. We may be Muslims, Jews, or Christians, but until our hearts become the mold for every heart we will see only our differences."[13]

"I am the Light of the World," was Jesus's doctrine when he lost his ego-self in his own divine heart flame.[14] He observed that when people touch right doctrine, they turn with it to look toward their own heart.

They do not despise their heart as a material illusion without reality. Instead, they look toward it as a point of light shining forth from their whole body.

They do not despise their heart as a mind center and thus only an instrument to use. Instead they look toward it as the one and only Light.

Therein they find their original form, their first beauty, their undimmed wisdom. They experience that they are indeed "children of God," "joint heirs with Christ," as the Hebrew and Christian scriptures say. They discover their pristine splendor as an extension and expression of the One, which is the spiritual meaning of "child of God." And so they find that their own heart is worthy of their full attention.

They keep their lamp burning by looking toward their own heart till they see within it all that it contains of the divine Fire. Then from that understanding, they're able to shed an unfailing light on the heavenly kingdom near them.

Saints and yogis of the past practiced sitting with their eyes turned toward their heart centers until it exposed their divine prototype as a being all glorious. At their first gaze, nothing was glorious; but with their steady gaze, it became glorious. At their first gaze, their own prototype seemed small; with their steady gaze, it became mighty and like a devouring flame. Into their heart all the worlds were able to merge. As Isaiah prophesied, "A little one shall become a thousand and a small one a great nation,"[15] and in their scriptures the yogis proclaimed, "Brahman is the smallest of the small and the greatest of the great."[16]

As all things far away seem small to the eyes, so our Emmanuel, the farthest away of all beings according to our senses, seems inconceivably small to anyone who thinks of looking within their own heart. Is not the heart regarded as a small organ that can perform many functions? But what if now the heart is found to be the chief and only organ we have?[17] What if the heart were so stupendous in its role that when anyone looks into it, they become no longer people of flesh and bones, but the transcendent Buddha, Christ, or Emmanuel? If this doctrine shines with any splendor for you, then you've made one more step away from the literal toward the spiritual.

Whoever understands their own heart understands the Everlasting. Those who look out toward the kingdom here at hand from the knowledge within their own heart also look from self to Self. The true light that Moses speaks of in the Book of Genesis then shines. Those people can say as Emmanuel, as Krishna, as Goddess Within, as the Great Spirit, "I am Om"; "I am the Light." They say, "I am Understanding." They speak as the One Everlasting, "The Kingdom is here, now."

BEING UNDERSTANDING

According to your heart you are either a seer of the all as One or a seer of the all as not One but many. The pure in heart see the Light and through it see the all as One. Let the many doctrines offer light as best they may, but only in your heart can you see it plainly.

You can let that light be plainly visible to you and all others when your heart is focused on one single divinity; the single eye is your heart. Your understanding heart shall see It. And you have as much understanding as you have heart in your religion.

All the world's scriptures are divine. Interpret them as divinity made manifest and see God by whatever name you call it.

All your body is divine. Interpret it as God and see Spirit unhindered. Nothing clings to Spirit and darkens it.

"The kingdom of God comes not by looking," said Jesus.[18] It comes only with the knowledge that as Omnipresence is in everything, everywhere, It is in us now, the pure unalterable One is who I Am. Let me be not deceived into conceiving any doctrine that's not of the heart.

Essential Points

- Whatever interpretation of scripture pleases you best is your doctrine, which is your illumination.
- The literal interpretation of the Bible, Qur'an, Bhagavad Gita, and other scriptures preaches a doctrine of death, torment, and distress.

- The mental interpretation of the world's scriptures can make you think that you must speak and think, "I decree," in order to have power and bring forth good.

- The spiritual understanding, the God interpretation, would show you that all you have to do is to be; you can find every object and every event an instrument for your use and enjoyment without any effort on your part.

- Understanding this, we see how it may be that someone steadily holding his or her own lamp of abundant provision in a city full of people who appear to be starving can cause the abundant provisions to be revealed to the populace while not stirring from chair.

- If your former doctrine said that difficult, hard labor was the lot and law of life, you may still find yourself struggling. If so, your "I decree" doctrine is not yet your hearty doctrine and you've not yet touched the doctrine of "let be."

- As we move forward in this Science, the realization comes that there's nothing to be created—all is created; nothing to be done—all is done. The "let be" doctrine will show that which Is: heavenly peace, Nirvana, Samadhi, Paradise.

- Those who look toward their own heart as a point of light shining forth through their whole body find their original form, their first beauty, their undimmed wisdom.

- You have as much understanding as you have heart in your religion.

- All the world's scriptures are divine. Interpret them as divinity made manifest and see God by whatever name you call it. All your body is divine; see it as Spirit unhindered.

Practicing the Principle

1. Each week, write out your own doctrine. If you're not sure what it is, look at how your life works for clues. The world around you is your doctrine made manifest. If you find that your doctrine includes ideas you no longer wish to hold, go back to lesson 2 for insights on how to let them go and replace them with Truth.

2. Each week, write about any experiences with transforming your own issues or other people's. Include any words you may have spoken (silently or aloud) for them and the results of doing so. If new ideas come to you in the process, write them down as well. These words are called treatments, and their effectiveness is enhanced when we write them as well as speak them.

LESSON 9
REMEMBERING

The great Hebrew rabbi Maimonides[1] was a wise scholar of sacred literature during the twelfth century. He said of the book of Genesis, "Whoever shall find out the true sense of the book of Genesis ought to take care not to divulge it. If a person should discover the true meaning of it by himself or by the aid of another, then they ought to be silent, or if they speak of it, they ought to speak of it only obscurely and in an enigmatical way."[2] Evidently, Maimonides knew that the book is a parable with a motif, telling important spiritual principles in figures of speech.

In our day, there are many who doubt that there ever were any such people mentioned in that book. It's been called by some a book written by intuitional memory. What is this memory? It's a way of bringing into the present moment something outside of our normal space and time. Consider, for example:

A child waking early one morning tried to remember where she had come from when she was born. She knew the memory was there but could not find it, and soon the sounds and sights of her earthly and familiar home caused her to forget that long past experience. Again, in middle life, came the same experience of trying to remember the memory of some wonderful and happy life before being born, but again, the memory faded before it was captured.[3]

Mathematicians, musicians, and others illustrate another form of this memory. Sometimes they suddenly realize that they're doing something they've done before, and that there are even more points about it that they realize they've already known. Others call these people and their works original and wonderful, but they know that they're simply remembering something outside of normal space and time.

Ezra, a Hebrew priest in about 460 BCE, used this kind of memory. He reached backward to some thought he held with the Creator-Source before the world was and told that knowledge in a story. Integrating many tales told around the fires of the Hebrew tribes over the centuries, he explained how the spiritual world is good and isn't capable of recognizing matter or evil, and described the power and splendor of the spirit of humanity. Then he wrote these ideas down in what became the first books of the Hebrew Bible.

In those stories he taught a lesson. Consider what he taught:

The spirit of humanity is able to multiply and replenish all that the human will is set to do. It's able to subdue its whole world, not by the labor of tilling the soil or building huge machines but by knowl - edge of Good only. In that knowledge, the human spirit finds everything desirable. In the realm of Spirit, nothing is dirty, scarce, or unreliable, but all is good throughout. The good corn never fails. The good gold is never scarce. Moreover, the good grain and gold have knowledge in themselves of how to move into the right places and are capable of speaking to the right people. They appear where the will is ready to receive them. Their substance is Wisdom.

This is the intuitional memory that Ezra brought forth, and the Spiritual interpretation of the Book of Genesis that rabbi Maimonides said we are to be careful of sharing.

THE HOME POINT, THE "I" AT OUR CENTER

The Hebrew scriptures say, "Remember now your Creator in the days of your youth."[4] Remember and remember until your mind touches the home point, the "I" at your center, now, before you put any more time into your imagination of what might be.

The apostle Paul said, "If they had only been mindful of the country from whence they came out."[5] All his practice was trying to be mindful of that inner country.

The great Sufi poet Rumi told us:

For ages you have come and gone
courting this delusion.
For ages you have run from the pain
and forfeited the ecstasy.
So come, return to the root of the root
of your own soul.[6]

All the meditations of the adepts of India are their endeavor to recollect their true nature and origin. All the original music, all the brilliant mathematics, all announcements of mighty truths are humanity's recollections of the original knowledge found at our central "I." All the struggles of the great thinkers are the endeavors of the ego-self mind to step backward to its home point.

That home point is in us, the "I" at the center of our being. There's nowhere we can go that we are not in our home. The Mind that is our home is an eternal, absolute point, the Eternal One.

HUMAN EXPERIENCE

All that we experience as humanity are our thoughts of what the all-in-all would be if we were something other than we truly Are. But those thoughts are not real and have no existence in Truth.

Consider how the material world came into being:

The divine Source of all, as Substance (or what we now call the quantum field), condescends to be matter by means of a thought. This everywhere-present field of Intelligence takes on individualized form in accordance with the thought—the beliefs and doctrines—held by the mind observing it. This thought, capable of comprehending all that is called earthly experience, has imagined instead what it would be like to be not powerful, to experience helpless ignorance, to be subject to time and change. It projects a universe based on lack and limitation and we call this imagining the nature of the world.

Whoever has imagined sin, let that person know its nature. Whoever has imagined poverty, let them know its nature. Both are simply ideas of lack imagined by the ego-self and brought into material form out of the divine Substance that is the Source of all. This world, with all its fear-filled strife, is imagined ideas, not reality.

And when people have had enough of such ideas, they may drop them. Then they will no longer experience life based on those ideas, and what is True may be to them as it was in the beginning, is now, and ever shall be.

As Rumi wrote, continuing the previously quoted poem:

Although you appear in earthly form
Your essence is pure Consciousness.
You are the fearless guardian
of Divine Light.
So come, return to the root of the root
of your own soul.[7]

Since everyone is an aspect of the One Source, what each has chosen to think and imagine was their privilege, their power, their ability. When they chose to imagine matter, they had the right, the freedom, and the power to do so. They had the right even to imagine what it would be to be dust. They also had the right to be an idea of the whole realm of what we call nature. Each person had the right to call him or herself Krishna or Christ, Miriam or Eve, Adam or John Doe.

And everyone has the right to cease calling themselves by any name other than their own true name and to recollect their majesty and bliss as Pure Beingness. This recollection is the goal of meditation and contemplation. It's the culmination of intuitional memory.

TRUE GENIUS

Genius is simply attention focused on one subject till the realization of something unusual is felt, then another realization, then another. It's a form of memory, like the intuitional memory described in this lesson. Those who've learned how to put their mind on one subject till it has revealed its hidden beauty in one new good after another are recollecting the true nature of that subject.

Discovery of music beyond Mozart's, Beethoven's, or Andrew Lloyd Webber's compositions will be only the mind recollecting its True Home. There, a divine Music can be heard and can be translated into a music discernible by the senses.

The Qur'an and all the Hindu sacred books were touches of this kind of memory. Read their history and see how their authors realized that they were not authors but memorizers and how, in order to learn to remember their own divinity, each mystic learned to remember every divine statement they could gather.

Writers and speakers who mix their imaginations of what it is to be poor, old, sick, or feeble with their statements of Truth are not operating from their home point. They're like politicians who cover their actual intentions with stories about their past accomplishments or musicians who cover themselves with sequins and rhinestones while performing sacred songs. The bling is not necessary. In fact, it distracts the listeners from the purity of the music and the power of the message. Neither are descriptions of poverty or pain essential to the religionists' statements of divinity, but religionists have distracted people for ages by acting as if they were an essential part of the message.

RECOLLECTING TOGETHER

It's each being's business to recollect the Mind at the center of our being. The Absolute Knower's unchangeable abode is the starting point of humanity, planet, animal, plant, and pebble alike. It's our true Home.

The pebble can remember as well as Ezra. When you find a piece of gold, it's the gold remembering its true nature and touching you on its homeward journey. When bags of money burst open on the highway, it's the truth of their nature to become rightfully distributed among humanity and move one step nearer their true Home. The stars hear the songs of people who are reminding them that all is divine and who gather up the dropped chords of their ages. The sands shine and smile while we repeat the story of the Home we came from and let their coverings of thought fall and expose their glistening hearts.

The thoughtful people of our planet are feeling the movement of the Spirit as we remind ourselves of who we were in the beginning, who we are now, and who we shall be forever. Together they sing,

> I came forth from the One Source.
> I know what is not That One and what Is.
> I know now that I am an aspect of that One,
> and knowing this again, leaving all else,
>   I am in my right Mind.

Essential Points

- All the meditations, all the original music, all the brilliant mathematics, all announcements of mighty truths are humanity's recollections of the original knowledge at our central "I."
- All the struggles of the great thinkers are the endeavors of the ego-self mind to step backward to its home point.
- That home point is in us. There's nowhere we can go that we are not in our home. The Mind that is our home is an absolute point, the Eternal One.
- All that we experience as human beings are our imaginings and dreams of what would be if we were not That. When humanity has had enough of such ideas, they may drop them, and what is True may be true to them as it was in the beginning, is now, and ever shall be.
- Since everyone is an aspect of the One Source, what they've chosen to think was their privilege, their power, their ability. When they chose to imagine matter, or even to be dust, they had the right.
- It's each being's business to recollect the Mind. The pebble can remember as well as the composer. When you find a piece of gold,

it's the gold remembering its true nature and touching you on its homeward journey.

• The thoughtful people of our planet are feeling the movement of the Spirit as we remind ourselves of who we were in the beginning, who we are now, and who we shall be forever.

Practicing the Principle

Consider one of the things you've attempted to make happen in your world. It may be a new or better relationship, better health or work, or a new or better home or community. How long was it before you saw results? If you're fretting because it seems to take a long time for your thoughts of good to be seen in your environment, repeat the following until it is a part of you:

"The Spirit that I Am is joyous and sings because Spirit *is* joy. Spirit, which I am, need never pray for joy nor beg for it, nor work for it, nor struggle for it. I am glad and appreciate that the Spirit that I Am is joy and harmony made manifest in my life and world—here, now, always, and everywhere."

LESSON 10
UNITY

A s the human, mortal mind turns its thoughts and speech toward the Divine Mind, we see a strange shining around the things in our world; we feel a strange power flowing in and around our bodies.

When the human mind touches the Absolute, it becomes a radiant thing, and people coming into the presence of such a mind are aware that something out of the ordinary is taking place.

Many a face glows because someone's attention has long been held toward the One Source. Many a speaker has startled listeners by their sudden eloquence because the mind has focused on the fire point where the Awesome Spirit lives and dies not. There, down in the deep heart of beingness, shines the fire point. There, at the central "I," where the mind begins, the fire point glows.

Great miracle workers have overwhelmed men and women with a nameless power streaming from their presence. They do so in some measure to this day, but too often the power seems to leave them when they spend too much time with other people or handle material things. This changing state means they must be approaching the Absolute only in their ritual of prayer, for their ego-self minds are not really in touch with the central "I" of power.

The face of Emanuel Swedenborg[1] shone so greatly after his midnight communing with the Absolute Mind that his servants grew frightened.

Moses spent thirty years in the mountains turning his thoughts entirely upon the everlasting, unquenchable God of his understanding. His power then became so great that when he lifted his hands for Pharaoh's army to stand back and not harm the Israelites, the Red Sea rolled back and the Israelites were able to walk safely across. Moses called that Eternal One by an unpronounceable name that is written as "the Lord." He knew that the Absolute Good works and none shall hinder it, so he said, "Stand ye still and see the salvation that the Lord will bring for you this day."[2]

Armies always march to victory when their generals touch the Absolute and Eternal Presence while their soldiers sleep. Mothers who turn toward the Changeless and Absolute send ships carrying their sons safely across stormy waters. Surgeons who spend a moment before an operation in silent communion with the Healing Presence have a higher success rate than their materialist peers. This is the fulfillment of the promise of the world's scriptures.

MANY WAYS

The human mind struggles to be born of divinity. But it makes no difference what process you use to turn the attention of your mind to the Very Present One; you can count on it that you shall touch God by your mind's sight. It's inevitable. When the human mind touches the Divine Mind, it no longer functions; this is the only death there is. Divine Mind appears instead; this is the only Life.

Then, regardless of your previous life, you shall experience the eternal fire of Life and Love for your reward. This is the meaning of the Hebrew David's hymn: "If I make my bed (of attention) in hell, You are there. If I ascend up into heaven, You are there."[3] It's what Rumi meant when he wrote,

You are a volume in the divine book
A mirror to the power that created the universe
Whatever you want, ask it of yourself
Whatever you're looking for can only be found
Inside of you.[4]

Pranayama is a practice in yoga of breathing deeply to touch the Eternal One at the point where the breath leaves off. There, where the breath extends itself, blazes the powerful Spirit. So breathing will lead your mind to the God Mind. Therefore, breathe, people! Breathe yourselves to the ego-mind-death so that Divine Mind may live in you and through you and by you and for you.[5]

Bring your attention earthward by breathing till normal thought dies in you so that your true Friend, the Lord in whom is everlasting Strength, may live in its place. "Greater love hath no one than this, that a man lay down his life for his friend."[6]

There's a practice of finding the strings of light that stretch through the quantum field by touching and testing all things eternal with the mind. As we do so, the strings that bind the atoms together harmonize and vibrate with our attention, and we begin to understand how they work together. Among the Hindus, these strings are called Indra's Net and are the means by which all things in the universe are connected. Among quantum physicists, they're a possible explanation as to why electrons that are too far apart to communicate act as if they were bound together, and why some experiments seem not to be limited by normal time and space.[7]

You can touch the strings of light with your attention till your small ego-self is dead and the infinite strings will live in its place—for they are the radiant beams that shine straight from the Absolute. Feeling yourself relaxing and resting your whole being on their strength, you are carried to your shining heaven while still in your body. You are one with God. You, too, can say, "The Father and I are One," as did the Nazarene in that moment of union.

THE MOMENT OF ONENESS

The ancient Hindus taught that at one supreme moment, by whatever path we've taken or process we've used, all actions are abandoned and the heart takes sanctuary with the Absolute, leaving the mortal mind behind. In that moment, we realize the Truth that we are that One and nothing less than that One. We experience the union of mind with Mind, heart with Sacred Heart.

Whenever anyone tries the practice of putting their thoughts to one theme alone, there comes a supreme moment when they understand that one theme. Understanding It, they are It. We call this mastery—at that point there's no separation between the master and the idea, art, or science; all is one seamless whole.

The Emmanuel presence, as Krishna tells Arjuna, who represents the seeking human mind, calls to us and says, "Abandoning all acts, take sanctuary with Me alone. I shall liberate you from all sins, so do not grieve."[8] The omnipotent Presence in, through, and as Jesus the Nazarene said, "Ask in my name," using the Hebrew and Aramaic word *shem* instead of our English word *name*—*shem* meaning "nature, character, essence," more than simply the sound of what someone is called. He was telling us to enter that Eternal Essence, which in Greek is called *Chrestos*, and in English, the Christ. The Dalai Lama and other Buddhists call this essence our Buddha Nature, that essence of us that knows we are One and One alone, experiencing no separation, distress, or suffering—only peace. The Sufis unite with the eternal Beloved.

At this point, the theme they've focused on has dissolved in their understanding. No words, no thoughts, no expressions about it are left. The Holy Fire of Beingness has burned the rest away, leaving only the Truth.

So it is that the mind that is focused on a divine word with a divine meaning must be burned away by the meaning of the word till only that which is undying, indestructible Substance is left. The word *God*, in whatever language, operates this way; focusing on the transcendent Source and Power of all being lifts one out of normal life and into that realm. The Emmanuel Name operates this way, whatever it is for you: Krishna, Christ, Blessed Mother Mary, Nature, Beloved, Jesu, Maitreya, Great Spirit. Any of these names has the power to replace and dissolve what Emerson called "our self-important trifles"[9] if they have that divine meaning for you. The words "I am" or "One Power" will do the same for some people.

At one moment, the full power within the word is experienced. Then all other words but it are meaningless—as if they had died. The dry sands of manifested thoughts disappear, and only the Spirit is visible. The fires burn to death that the deathless fires of the One may be seen. The mind of humanity wishes to die so the Absolute Mind will be left.

Those who see all the actions of nature as all things visible breaking down and absorbing as simple physical matter into their environment are aware that they themselves, at their central point, are indissoluble. They see then that all things have their indissoluble center point. The undying spirit of the brook as it runs to dissolve into the ocean, the undying substance of the fire as it consumes its own fuel—all are One at the center.

This awareness fixes the attention of our minds on that center, which we come to realize is the Divine Mind. The individual focuses on the undividable and thereby becomes aware that there is One alone and that all mind is that One. There is no separation, no distance at all.

In that moment, in the same way that we stretch our bodies on awakening in the morning, the individual mind arouses itself. And in that moment it illuminates Omnipresence. Then we see that there is nothing but the God Mind, no home to go to because Home is here now.

Rumi said, "My friend, you thought you lost Him; that all your life you've been separated from Him. Filled with wonder, you've always looked outside for Him, and haven't searched within your own house."[10]

Wherever you look, it is that God Center attracting you. Whatever you feel called to do, it is to recollect that Presence within.

Knowing these two truths—that each center is the God that attracts you and that it is your own God center that is attracted—you know all that is to be known.

THE UNREALITY OF THE MATERIAL WORLD

That which seems to be matter is dissolved by this knowledge. That which seems to be evil is dissolved by this knowledge. That which seems to be ignorance is dissolved by this knowledge. In this way, that which was written of knowledge comes to pass: "Ye shall know the truth and the truth shall make you free."[11]

The only truth to know of matter is that it has no reality of its own, for Spirit is all. "Matter consists in extension," said Spinoza.[12] "The field governs the particle," said Einstein late in his life. "Matter is the result of consciousness," say modern physicists Fred Alan Wolf and Amit Goswami.

This means that the whole realm of matter is supposition. All our world is the unfolding of the suppositions of our minds. Suppose you had a million dollars. Suppose there were a war or a new technology or a new government. Suppose you were Spirit, free and wise, and should for one instant imagine yourself bound in matter. Suppose you saw all the free Spirit of the universe as a mass of ignorance needing instructions. Do any of these suppositions make Reality any different?

At my undefeatable central point, I realize I am the Absolute. When I spend my nights focusing my attention on the undefeatable Absolute in the universe, I am laying aside suppositions. I am showing my Self to myself. And those who know the Self know all.

It's no wonder that miracles are wrought by those who know how, by any process whatsoever, to lay off suppositions and strike back upon knowledge!

The choice to know Truth or to suppose a world of matter and its processes is yours. Covering yourself with suppositions, you can only experience earthly conditions. Uncovering your original knowledge, you will transcend. The Self that you are shines over and transforms all things.

Essential Points

• When the human mind touches the Absolute, it becomes a radiant thing, and people coming into the presence of such a mind are aware of something out of the ordinary having taken place.

- It makes no difference what process you use to turn the attention of your mind to the Very Present One. You can count on it that you shall touch God by your mind's sight. It's inevitable.

- There's a practice of breathing deeply to touch the Eternal One at the point where the breath leaves off. There, where the breath extends itself, blazes the powerful Spirit. So breathing will lead your mind to the God Mind.

- The mind focused on a divine word with a divine meaning is burned away by the meaning of the word till only that which is undying, indestructible Substance is left. The word *God*, in whatever language, operates this way; the Emmanuel Name operates this way, as well, whatever it is for you.

- Knowing that each center is the God that attracts you and that it is your own God center that is attracted, you know all that is to be known.

- "Matter is the result of consciousness," say modern physicists. This means that the whole realm of matter is supposition. All our world is the unfolding of the suppositions of our minds.

Practicing the Principle

Take one afternoon each week to regard one of your neighbors with your heart, in your hidden meeting place with divinity, seeing the health and well-being that is that person's Truth. Also, take the people you love best into that place and do the same. This is a treatment.

If you will take your practice period to say all that the Spirit does not believe and all that the Spirit does believe, you will not have a long treatment with whoever or whatever your case—whether you are treating yourself or another. Try these words:

"I have not believed in a mixture of good and evil. I do not believe in evil of any kind; I believe that all is Good. There is no reality in trouble; all is peace. There is no reality in sickness; all is perfect health. I do not believe in anything wrong; I believe all is well."

LESSON 11
INTELLIGENCE AND WISDOM

People who are blind train their ears and fingers to be their eyes for them. People who are born deaf train their eyes, skin, and muscles, their bones and nerves, to be ears. They expand the ways they use the always-present Intelligence.

BRAIN DEVELOPMENT

It was discovered in the mid-1800s that the brain transfers some of its ganglionic cells to the fingers and toes of blind people. In the late twentieth century, neurologists found similar cells gathered in the heart. By this generous sharing, all humanity can see that intelligence dwells not in the brain only, nor is intelligence dependent upon the brain, but is spread wherever it is useful.

Brain tissue can't separate and distribute itself. It's clearly subservient to some form of intelligence, and its tissue is generated or not generated according to that intelligence.

This is one of many indications that the brain is not the source and seat of intelligence but actually a sort of receiver/transmitter. It receives intelligence from an unlimited, nonlocal source in the form of visual, harmonic, and symbolic information, and transmits it to various centers in the body through the release of chemicals and electrical impulses. Different areas of the brain are responsible for different kinds of signals, but they are neither the source nor the integrator of those signals. As such, the brain is simply a tool or instrument available for our use, albeit a powerful one.

It's curious that people have concerned themselves so much with the instruments they use and so little with the source of these instruments. It's clear that the maker of an instrument must know how to multiply and replenish it many times over; therefore, if people could get into the good graces of the intelligence that forms and manages brain tissue, they might be able to bring some undreamed-of powers, inventions, and other helpful possibilities to the attention of the rest of humanity.

LIGHT AND SHADOW

The Hindus have taught for thousands of years that there's a luminous spot in the brain that governs the head and body. Yogis say that watching it steadfastly with one's inner vision will give one the power to see divine beings.[1] They've taught that only at this luminous spot in the brain can some mighty Spiritual Sun—unseen by the eyes of humanity, unheard by their ears, untouched by their fingers—be seen. So as the physical body is warmed, invigorated, and strengthened by the sun, this luminous spot, which manages the head and body, is renewed and strengthened by the Spiritual Sun, feeling its warmth and moving in its smile. This, it appears, is the reason so many spiritual traditions use an image of the sun to represent the Source of life.

This luminous spot that the ancient Hindus described is not only the manager but the source, the maker of the gray matter we call the brain and its ganglionic cells. In modern neural research, the cell maker is a deeply buried part of the brain in which "a small region of the hippocampus known as the *dentate gyrus*, a brain structure needed for memory and learning . . . is home to the subgranular zone . . . where neural stem cells continue to produce the precursor cells that ultimately differentiate into neurons."[2]

We've all experienced playing with our shadow in the bright sunlight. Shadows are formed when matter is in the presence of light. In the same way, matter is formed when Spiritual Substance (which modern scientists call the quantum field) is in the presence of Spiritual Light (intelligent awareness).

In the Hindu tradition, gray matter is described as developing in the brain as the shadow of light received from the inner Spiritual Sun. In modern neural research, this light is observed as "enriched environment"—that is, awareness of opportunities to learn and discover. In a series of experiments over the past several decades, "the brains of mice housed in enriched environments produced far more neurons."[3]

In the Hindu tradition, if the luminous spot receives only a little light from the Spiritual Sun, it casts only a little shade of itself and so develops only a little gray matter. There is then only a little character, only a little sense of value in the person. When individuals focus their inner sight on that luminous spot or on the Light beyond it, then a larger shadow is cast and more gray matter is formed. We call such people wise and powerful.

In the Western tradition, this process begins with the ancient Greek directive: "Know Thyself." As people truly begin to understand their nature and potential, their minds expand to include all the intelligence of the body and beyond. We call such people geniuses and mystics.

DISAPPEARANCE OF THE SHADOW

Sometimes lights shine on us from all directions and our shadow is gone; the Substance is alone in the light, absorbing it from all directions. If the luminous spot in the brain is the substance that casts the shadow called gray matter, then when the Spiritual Sun shines on it from every direction there can be no more gray matter, no more flesh, and neither great nor small character. Nor can there be any worthy or unworthy will or even sense. There is nothing to be called good or not good. All is the Light.

The brain's gray matter disappears when it is absorbed in the luminous spot, its manager, just as the luminous spot disappears when it is absorbed in the Spiritual Sun, its manager. It follows, then, that the Spiritual Sun itself disappears when it is absorbed in the One Starting Point of all that moves or stands still.

The body is under the management of the brain's gray matter, that gray matter is under the management of the luminous spot we find within it, that luminous spot is under the management of the Spiritual Sun, and the Spiritual Sun is under the management of the unnamed Origin, the Starting Point of all. It's then clear that our only useful activity is to look utterly and continually toward the Starting Point of all that is. This is the message of the Roman catechism that states, "We are here to love and serve God." It's the essence of the injunction found in the scriptures of Jews, Christians, and Muslims alike: "Pray unceasingly."

That Starting Point is the Substance that casts the shadows of matter we give so many names to, but It has only one name, indescribable in any language: "that which can be named is not the Tao"; "the name of the Lord shall not be spoken." It is the One Mind, the ground of being from which all thought, all form emerges. All other mind is mere supposition.

It's plain that any other mind but It is supposition because everything that any other mind tells its body or its senses to do is an experiment. Do musicians positively know that their fingers will perform at the concert hall? Do they positively know their head will keep level and not get rattled? Do motivational speakers or stand-up comics positively know that their thoughts will charm and magnetize their audience? Not even the most brilliant mathematicians are positive they will not blunder. All is supposition, and it all vanishes from the memory of the most enrapt listener and observer after a few days.

HEARING THE VOICE

There's a new tide of thought springing forth from humanity's recent discovery that the suppositional life is not worth living. "What makes life worthwhile?" so many cry. And in their crying they do not hear the voice that has always been there.

Listen: "I am, and there is none beside me."[4] These are the words that stream from the One at the Starting Point. This is Om. This is the voice of the angels transmitting the constant refrain of the Eternal.

That voice says, "You have not known Me. You have supposed something not Me." It tells us, "The world is the picture of your thoughts which you have suppressed," reminding us that what we see is what we project onto the changeable quantum field around and through us. Modern science confirms this, telling us that matter forms only in the presence of an observer. The Sufi teacher Rumi said "This place is a dream. Only a sleeper considers it real. Then death comes like dawn, and you wake up laughing at what you thought was your grief."[5]

"Nature has no actuality. You are Nature's painter." This is the essence of Ralph Waldo Emerson's discovery and message. You have laid your suppositions on the changing substance of this world, and so take a good look at the trees and rocks and stars. What an artist you can be!

And when we stop painting and enter the silence again, we hear the still, small voice within saying, "Your picture shall be what you call forth while you focus on it and then it shall be resolved back into nothingness when you look toward Me." Again, modern science confirms this: without an observer bringing forth matter, all that is remains formless, immeasurable.

"When you speak well of My Goodness and majesty, you are Emmanuel," that voice whispers, reminding us of who we were born to be. This is the goal of the spiritual traditions: "Praise the Lord O my Soul!" sings the obedient shepherd David in the Psalms. "Give thanks and praise in all you do," says the apostle Paul in his letters. "Honor the Great Spirit at sunrise and sunset, and all through the day," say the Native American elders. "All thanks unto Allah," repeat the followers of Mohammed.

And so we fill our hearts and minds and begin to live the Good and Truth and Wisdom we seek.

BEYOND WORDS

But the voice goes further: "When you no longer speak well of My majesty and goodness, but see Me as I am, you have a science higher than words." The Emmanuel Name that evokes our awareness of Omnipresent Omnipotence is the highest we can imagine of majesty and goodness. It transcends, is free from, the spoken word.

Giving up words, the Emmanuel Mind sees goodness, majesty, and loveliness. The world is transformed into a new place of peace, which is the meaning of the "new Jerusalem" that John describes in the Book of Revelation. With him we see "a new heaven and a new earth"; the veil has been lifted; the apocalypse (a Greek word that means "lifting the veil") is complete.

Then, when goodness, majesty, and loveliness have wrought their highest mission, they also cease and that which is independent of all states appears. All is Light. All is One. This is the eternal splendor that people, having found it, lose themselves in as they find it. It's Nirvana, Samadhi, the Eternal Now.

The air around those who lose themselves this way is filled with divine aroma. It's the always present, all-pervading Wisdom. They breathe the breath of it and become the aroma. It is the breath that the ancients knew would make one God if they breathed.

They become the living One; Spirit; the Wonderful Light that all things else are shadows of; the One Intelligence all other intelligences are suppositions of; the One Word; the One Name that sustains the universe that all spoken, written, or even thought of names are symbols of.

This Science we've been studying is the Science of Good and Truth, but the Science the Emmanuel Mind knows is the Science of the Unspoken Word, the One Name that fills the universe, of whom even Good and Truth are simply symbols.

It's the One Substance, the One Intelligence that governs all things. It is the Eternal Refuge, the Everlasting Creative Power, the Absolute Wisdom, the glorious Intelligence everywhere One.

Whatsoever is not This is not at all.

Essential Points

- Intelligence manages the brain, which acts as intelligence but is only an instrument.

- Shadows are formed when matter is in the presence of light. The maker of a shadow is the substance that casts it, so matter is formed when Spiritual Substance (the quantum field) is in the presence of Spiritual Light (intelligent awareness).

- When individuals focus their inner sight on the luminous spot at the center of the brain or on the Light beyond it, then a larger shadow is cast and more gray matter is formed. We call such people wise and powerful.

- If the body is under the management of the brain, that gray matter is under the management of the luminous spot within it, the luminous spot is under the management of the Spiritual Sun, and the Spiritual Sun is under the management of the unnamed Origin of all. It's then clear that our only useful activity is to look utterly and continually toward the Origin of all that is for the management of all our experience.

- "I am, and there is none beside me" are the words that stream from the One at the Starting Point. This is Om. This is the voice of the angels transmitting the constant refrain of the Eternal.

- That voice says, "You have not known Me. You have supposed something not Me. The world is the picture of your thoughts which you have suppressed," reminding us that what we see is what we project onto the changeable quantum field.

- That voice says, "Your picture shall be all that you call forth while you focus on it, then resolved back into nothingness when you look toward Me."

- The Emmanuel Name that evokes our awareness of Omnipresent Omnipotence is the highest we can imagine of majesty and goodness. It transcends, is free from, the spoken word, so the Emmanuel Mind sees only goodness, majesty, loveliness—no other possibility exists.

- Then when goodness, majesty, and loveliness have fulfilled their highest mission, they also cease, and All is Light. All is One. The Eternal Now of love-bliss-consciousness is all.

Practicing the Principle

1. **Releasing and replacing.** Every few months (at the turn of the seasons, for example, or between terms at school), consider your life for six days, speaking of your own spiritual nature as it was at the time of your conception. Take each year of your life and deny that there are any causes or results of causes in you or around you that could lead to any experience of disease, poverty, distress, or failure. Write down your new description of your life and being, free of all discord and disharmony. Review it and revise it every few months. You may do the same for family members.

2. **Filling the mind.** Mark a period of at least twenty-eight days on your calendar as a time to fill your thoughts and world with praise and thanksgiving.

   a. If you're a Muslim, you can use this exercise to take the month of Ramadan to a new level. If you're a Jew, extend the High Holy days to the whole month of Nissan. If your background is Christian, you might use Lent or Advent or the period between the Resurrection and Pentecost. (These Christian seasons are forty days or more, but they fit the religious calendar we're accustomed to.) If your path is earth centered, use a full moon cycle for this process.

   b. Create a set of reminders of what you want to be thinking and saying. You can write them on sticky notes or on your screensaver, or you can use a dry-erase marker on a whiteboard, window, or mirror, or chalk on a chalkboard, or print up some index cards or business cards—or all of the above! Fill them with words of praise, thanks, love, and appreciation for the Infinite Love, Support, and Supply that is now and always has been present in your life.

   c. For these days, set a timer to chime every fifteen minutes (one of those clocks that bongs on the quarter hour could work—that's actually why they were made that way—or your cell phone, computer, or oven timer) to remind you to stop whatever you're doing and focus your attention on the Highest Source of All that is.

d. As you prepare for bed at night and get ready to go out in the morning, repeat some of the words you've written.

e. As you drink or eat anything, repeat some of the words you've written.

f. Take an hour every day just to focus your attention on the Highest Source of All. The hour can be in one block or divided into two or three sessions.

g. On the first day, on the days you take as a Sabbath, and on the last day of this period, write a description of what your life is like and what seems worthwhile about it. You can do this in your journal, on a blog, in an email, or whatever way allows you to record your thoughts and feelings.

h. At the end of the period, review your journals and decide how you want to be living. How much of this practice do you want to continue? Write it in the same place as you wrote your other descriptions.

i. Make a commitment to follow your new way for at least a season or school term (three to four months) and then review again.

j. If you're really serious about transforming your life and world, make a commitment to your new way of living for at least a year. This will not be a permanent pattern but will lead you toward your "New Jerusalem," after which you will be at one with the One you've been praising.

LESSON 12
FREEDOM

This plane of existence is one of loving and not loving. It's the plane of ideas and their demonstrations. In this plane, when we are loved, we are loved for our actions and behaviors, which are based on ideas both consciously and unconsciously held. When we are disliked, we are disliked for our ideas consciously or unconsciously held.

An idea not yet worked out into practice is a theory. When it's worked out into blood and bones, it is usefulness. Those who choose the usefulness of blood and bones accuse those who adhere to theories of not living their lives. Those who choose theories accuse the adherents of bones and blood of living their lives too much in the material.

Usefulness is demonstration, and some people say that a statement is not worth anything until it's made into health and a meal. Some people say that a statement is a truth to adore whether it has cured the body or not, whether it has fed the masses or not. And regardless of what they say, they all rejoice when a hundred-dollar bill arrives in their hands.

They would not say a word in any direction if they were utterly free.

The only difference between the religionist (of whatever creed) and the gangster is that the gangster will use and appreciate whatever is achieved by scheming, persuading, or killing, while the religionist will crush the ideas achieved by the same activities. Neither is free.

Those standing calmly and coolly by this battle of uses and theories touch them not but remain utterly detached from money, drugs, religious principle, or people who wrangle and know them for what they are. Such people also know themselves as they are; they know themselves as free from either. Only they are secure. Only they are free. This is the freedom that the Buddha and the Christ taught.

Security is the aim of the adherents of both theories and uses. Security means being out of reach of distress, out of reach of necessity, out of reach of contention, out of reach of effort. To achieve this, we must leave the plane of duality and enter the One. The Sufi mystic Rumi understood this:

My place is the Placeless, my trace is the Traceless;
'Tis neither body nor soul, for I belong to the soul of the
  Beloved.
I have put duality away, I have seen that the two worlds
  are one;
One I seek, One I know, One I see, One I call.[1]

The doctrine of the One is entirely of security. Becoming the "secure one" is the theme of all spiritual teachings. The greatest teachers are those who *become* the Emmanuel, the secure Immortal Mind not entangled with food, money, demonstrations of usefulness, or religious ideas. The Buddha said that the one secure from distress is the unattached one. This is true; the completely secure one has left behind being an adherent to any idea, thing, teaching, or philosophy.

By giving up all tendencies to adhere, you can be unburdened sufficiently to turn around and face your Secure Self. Our Secure Self is the one that the prophets, the priests, the millionaires, the presidents, and the players are all squabbling to be, though they may not understand that this is so.

Realizing this, we find ourselves saying as a closing prayer,

Oh, You, Mighty One! I see that You are not reached by effort. You are reached by facing you, released from efforts.

You don't need to toil and labor. You don't need to use money. You don't need to use religion. You don't need to be praised. You don't need to be watching out for opportunities to cut your way through squabbling money grabbers or squabbling religionists. You don't need to make your living. You have no debts to pay. You have no position to hold. You have nothing to hold. You don't need a thing.

Wonderful One! How easy it is to envy you! This is the envy that reaches security. I, by envying Your unattached indifference, become secure.

You are the One I am jealous of, for You sit on that throne that I have been squabbling with others over ideas and hands to secure. This is the jealousy—the only jealousy—that reaches security, for it keeps me watching You; and watching You, I become one with You. This is the only malice that reaches security, for it keeps me watching You. Anything that keeps me watching You frees me from all attachments. It's a sight of security to watch You, though I watch You by fighting You, for it makes me forget money and people and religion. I remember only You.

I see you while I fight you, and I fight You for Your security. And like Jacob, "I will not let you go except You bless me." Give it to me. If I have contention, it shall be with You. Why squabble with anyone else for that which they don't have? You, the Source of all being, have what I've panted after since before time.

To look toward You is to secure Your security. Have You not always spoken, "Turn unto Me"? See! I wrestle with You, Secure One. I am after all that You are and have. I will not let You go except You give me You as my Self.

Then and only then will I be secure. Then and only then will I know peace. Then and only then will I rise

above this world and experience Your creation. And "then" need not be some time in the future, for in You all time is now. So be it.*

When this, or something like this, becomes our constant prayer, then and only then will we rise above the dual nature of this plane of existence and be free.

Essential Points

- This plane of existence is one of loving and not loving. It's the plane of ideas and their demonstrations.
- Those who stand calmly and coolly by the tension of dualities and touch them not but remain utterly detached know them for what they are.
- The greatest teachers are those who become the Emmanuel, the secure Immortal Mind not entangled with food, money, demonstrations of usefulness, or religious ideas.
- Such people also know themselves as they are; they know themselves as free from duality of all kinds. Only they are secure.

Practicing the Principle

1. The final affirmation of this Science is, "Knowing all things and doing all things, I am independent of all things. I am absolutely free!" Repeat it until it becomes your own.
2. Take part of each Sabbath day alone and write or speak (internally) to some usually unreachable person in your world. This person may be someone from your past or someone you would not normally come into contact with but whose thoughts and actions affect your world. You need not send the letter or share the words with anyone, for the thoughts of your heart will touch them. Remind them of the Truth of their being, communing with the Absolute who sees only the Good in each of us. Do so knowing that this communication makes a difference in your world and theirs.

---

*Adapted and updated from Hopkins's own words. For the original quote, see pages 218–219.

LESSON SUMMARIES

Lesson 1: The first lesson gives us the foundational idea of the mind. It's the Statement of Being, that which IS. It finds out what your mind is seeking and names it. Aren't you seeking Good? Why do you move your right hand? You move it to get your Good. Why do you breathe? You breathe to get your Good. Why do the stones lie still and wait? They're waiting for their Good. Everything moves or waits for its Good. So you see that the Good you and I want governs everything we do. Therefore, the Good you've been seeking is your God. Health is God; Life is God; Supply is God. And since it is all the power of our lives, our God must be omnipotent; since it's everywhere we turn, it's omnipresent; and since it is the intelligence by which we think and choose, it is omniscient. *All that I call my Good is my God: Omni - present, Omnipotent, Omniscient.*

Lesson 2: Whenever the statement of what is true is called to our attention, we're able to see what is not true, so the second lesson is negation or denial. People rarely talk about the idea of where their Good is, while they frequently talk about their Good being absent. *I tell you that all that stands between you and your Good, which belongs to you and which you ought to have, is your own idea of the absence of Good in your life.*

Five general negating statements apply to the collective human consciousness; as we deny their reality, we are freed from the sense of separation they're built on. Two particular negating statements apply to each individual, addressing each person's own moral character and delighting their heart. As we negate our special prejudices, sickness falls away. Death hurries away like a dream. Sin and distressing behavior fall from other peoples' characters, and they don't seem the same to us anymore. We do not need to wait to be free. *As what we call God is free now, so we are free—here, now, and forever.*

Lesson 3: Mind and conditions follow the inner vision, so as we release the ideas that have blocked our vision, we can embody whatever we focus on continually. When the right negations are stated, our affirmations are exceedingly effective. Is anyone poor? They shall be poor no longer if they simply put themselves into the Owner of all, the creative Source of the universe. Likewise sickness. Prosperity comes from the acknowledgment, felt either consciously or unconsciously, of the presence of our Good. We release the ideas that we are separate from our Good and experience more Good in their place. This is the forgiveness ("giving-for-ness") that awaits us. *We turn our vision toward the One that is all Good until our lives are filled with it.*

Lesson 4: Faith is confidence to command, as in "give us this day . . ." Jesus the Nazarene didn't say, "According to your denials and affirmations be it unto thee"; rather, he said, "According to your faith be it unto thee." What we believe deep down inside is our faith, so to generate Faith, we do nothing but speak the Truth and stand to it. If we feel confident one moment that all will come out right and then our heart sinks the next moment because a bad appearance sets in, we are believing based on appearances rather than Faith. Our lives show what we have faith in, so we must have faith in the Good making our life conditions just right for us, no matter what seems to be operating against us. If there's turmoil in your life, it's a signal that you've tried to believe in the possibility of evil and the omnipresence of Good at the same time. It can't be done. Use this statement: *I believe that only the Good rules in and with my life. I have true Faith.*

Lesson 5: After the mind has been firm, our beliefs show up in the matter around us. "According to your faith be it unto thee" is a constantly working principle, which means that what we believe is always manifest in our bodies and our world. Our words make our faith the working principle, and our words in the silence of our minds are as powerful as our spoken, audible words. When we think according to these twelve lessons, our experience of our world comes closer to the original creation, the Reality of Good. The Real world is not changed by our words or thoughts; it's the same changeless Good yesterday, today, and forever. All our faith and all our reasoning simply open our eyes to the Real world. So we have nothing to do, for in Reality, all is, was, and ever shall be perfect. *The highest working power is the power to see that we have nothing to do.*

Lesson 6: There comes a moment when the full power of the words comes surging through us. The power isn't the words themselves; it comes *through* the words, and the power *is* the Reality. The word is a pathway to the power, and this power is the Secret of the Lord. We say, "God (Allah, Brahman, Beloved, Christ, Father, Krishna, Mother, Om, Presence, Spirit . . .) is all." Anything that is not the One we call God can't and doesn't exist. So if I exist, must I not be that One? And then that appearance of me that is not good is nothing. The moment I feel that truth, the world I've known dissolves into the peace, beauty, and wholeness of Reality, and the ego-mind discovers the security and love of the One. *We think, we write, and we speak words of power, and they are cast firmly in the world of appearances, dissolving the appearances into Reality.*

Lesson 7: We keep the words of Truth going continually: they change our life and increase our powers. Why would you say that you feel unhappy if saying this shuts the gate against the breath of the spirit? You are a miracle worker by inherent right. Give your soul, the divine essence of your being, the chance to do all your thinking, all your speaking. You may sometimes find yourself seeming to be sick. If so, then you have caught some of the world's false beliefs, or maybe some old notions you used to think are showing themselves. *No disease or distress comes from material causes, though the world may speak as if they do. All is in thought first.*

Lesson 8: Spirit never deceives. Matter is the only deceiver, being formulated by thoughts concerning a kind of God who never existed. We look at others through the filter of our own ideas, and we see them entirely different from what they are in reality. This means that what we describe as their character is not the truth about them; it must be in our own mind in some way. This is why the righteous are strangely afflicted; when we get the consequences that we believe should be someone else's, we are astonished and grieved and feel much abused. So the eighth lesson is: *"Be not deceived," either in humanity or in the nature of divinity, for both, in truth, are Good.* We address the issues we see in the world by changing the ideas in our mind, and we leave the world alone to dissolve into the Good we know to be the only Reality.

Lesson 9: The world we live in is an exact record of our thoughts and gives us exactly the experience we have called forth through our descriptions. Therefore, we do not accuse ourselves or anyone else of error, condemnation, or being ignorant or foolish. We realize that our ego-self does not do the works we see in the world; it is the One Mind within us that does them, responding to our description of how the world is. *We choose the Good, so we dwell in "I am satisfied" in joyful delight.* Then, the joyous heart being a healing presence, wherever we go, people are healed and distress dissolves into the Reality of Good.

Lesson 10: We must see the Good even where others may see evil. When it seems others' opinions are stronger than our faith, we stop all downward viewing and look only to the One. We ignore distressing appearances as the product of imagination and drive on with our principle as the expression of Truth. We begin to teach others to do what we can do, and so our works become permanent. *No matter what adversities face us, they are dissolvable if we remain true to our inner vision and inner words and allow the One to become our only experience.*

Lesson 11: When we've accepted the statements of Truth presented thus far, we have the ability to perceive Truth in all circumstances. Our perfect discernment, the marriage of meekness and will, touches the life chord of each situation so that all illusion is dissolved. *We refuse to admit that there is any foolishness, ignorance, weakness, old age, or failure in our Good, which is Reality.* This seeing through divine eyes dissolves all appearances unlike Good and is called perfect Judgment.

Lesson 12: Love casts out all fear. Our loving focus on the One lifts us above all attachments and opinions. It is great happiness, freedom! It's effortless achievement. It fills the mind and overflows to the world, awakening the same Love to shine back through all people and circumstances. No more grieving, no more hurting—forever! We dwell only in Love, meditate upon Love, and greet everything and everybody with goodwill, which is another name for Love. *We now see that there is nothing for us to do; we are the One we've been seeking; all is Good.*

NOTES

A NOTE FROM THE EDITOR

1. Shinn's book was published in 1925 and is still in print. It's also part of the Library of Hidden Knowledge series. *The New Game of Life and How to Play It: The Original Text by Florence Scovel Shinn,* ed. Ruth L. Miller (New York: Atria Books, 2012).

2. The exercises in this book are based on exercises Hopkins offered in other texts, including *Scientific Christian Mental Practice, High Mysticism,* and *Resumé: Studies in High Mysticism.*

3. Hopkins recommended specific practices that support each lesson to be done mornings and afternoons. These are presented in detail in Ruth L. Miller, *Unveiling Your Hidden Power: Emma Curtis Hopkins' Metaphysics for the 21st century* (Beaverton, OR: WiseWoman Press, 2005).

4. In nineteenth-century United States, Sunday was generally treated as a Sabbath day, a day to be set aside for communion with the divine, with Monday as the first day of the week. Hopkins suggested that on the Sabbath we meditate, pray, and contemplate, going, as the Christian New Testament suggests, "into our closet" to commune or celebrate with others the presence of Good in our world and our Oneness with the Source of All that Is.

   Times have changed, more people honor other days as the Sabbath, and readers are free to practice lesson 7 on whatever day they wish.

Introduction

1. For more detailed biographies, see Gail M. Harley, *Emma Curtis Hopkins: Forgotten Founder of New Thought* (Syracuse, NY: Syracuse University Press, 2002); and Ruth L. Miller, *Power to Heal: Emma Curtis Hopkins* (Beaverton, OR: Wise-Woman Press, 2010).
2. Harley, *Emma Curtis Hopkins: Forgotten Founder of New Thought*, 24.
3. Emma Curtis Hopkins, *Class Lessons of 1888*, Vancouver, WA: WiseWoman Press, 2008.
4. For a series of letters between Luhan and Hopkins that gives remarkable insights into their lives and time, see Mabel Dodge Luhan, *Movers and Shakers* (Albuquerque: University of New Mexico Press, 1985).
5. Luhan, *Movers and Shakers*, 470.

Lesson 1

1. David Bohm, *Wholeness and the Implicate Order*, reissue ed. (New York: Routledge, 2002).
2. Because this idea is part of its foundation, New Thought is often called "Neo-Platonism."
3. *Wormhole* is a popular term for the theory formally called an Einstein-Rosen Bridge. It's used in science fiction—most popularly in the *Star Trek* series—to describe a gateway through the fabric of space and time into other dimensions and infinite possibilities.
4. Psalms 1 10:1 (New International Version).
5. This story was not in the original text of *Esoteric Philosophy*. Hopkins tells about the incident in the third person in *High Mysticism*, Lesson Four; her student Marge Flotron, who lived in Chicago and maintained the High Watch Fellowship records until passing on in 2006, referred to it as Hopkins's own experience in an unpublished letter describing the difference between the DeVorss version of the book and others.
6. This is the first of the twelve stones that Hopkins associates with her lessons. They are the stones described as the foundation of the New Jerusalem in the Book of Revelation, and she uses them as metaphors for the foundation of our own new "Place of Peace," which is what the Hebrew word *Jerusalem* means.
7. 2 Kings 4:1–7 (NIV).
8. Acts 3:1–16 (NIV).

9. This research is described in David R. Hawkins's books *The Eye of the I: From Which Nothing Is Hidden* (West Sedona, AZ: Veritas, 2001); and *Power vs. Force: The Hidden Determinants of Human Behavior* (Carlsbad, CA: Hay House, 2002).
10. Genesis 39:4–6 (NIV).
11. Luke 10:38–42 (NIV).
12. Ibid., 17:21.
13. Ibid., 11:2.
14. This is the editor's translation from the original Aramaic of what some call "the prayer that Y'shua taught." Examples of the New Testament in Aramaic are widely available, including the following: Aramaic English New Testament, 5th ed., trans. Andrew Gabriel Roth (Mount Vernon, WA: Netzari Press, 2013).

LESSON 2

1. Isaiah 24:19 (NIV).
2. Matthew 10:34 (NIV).
3. Carlos Castaneda, *The Teachings of Don Juan: A Yaqui Way of Knowledge* (New York: Simon and Schuster, 1973). See also other books by Casteneda, esp. *A Separate Reality* (New York: Simon and Schuster, 1971).
4. Matthew 5:3 (NIV).
5. Psalms 110:1 (NIV).
6. Song of Solomon 1:3 (NIV).
7. Proverbs 16:10 (NIV).
8. John 10:18 (NIV).

LESSON 3

1. Joel 2:25 (NIV).
2. Bhagavad Gita 9:9 (Sivananda trans.).
3. Isaiah 45:22 (NIV).

LESSON 4

1. Emerson's essay "Nature" explores this idea in great detail. It's also woven into "The Oversoul" and "History."
2. Job 22:28 (NIV).
3. James 5:15 (NIV).

4. Foundation for Inner Peace, *A Course in Miracles: Combined Volume* (Mill Valley, CA: Foundation for Inner Peace, 2007).

5. For a summary of this research, see Robert Bruce Newman and Ruth L. Miller, *Empowered Care: Mind-Body Medicine Methods* (Newport, OR: Medigrace/Portal Center Press, 2012).

6. 1 Corinthians 15:51 (NIV).

7. Romans 12:2 (NIV).

8. *The Vedanta*, translated by Chunder Roo, first appearing in English in Israel Smith Clare, *Library of Universal History, Vol 2 Ancient Oriental Nations and Greece* (New York: Peale, 1897), 300.

9. Genesis 1:6 (NIV).

10. Hebrews 11:1 (NIV).

LESSON 5

1. Annie Besant, *An Introduction to Yoga: Four Lectures Delivered at the 32nd Anniversary of the Theosophical Society* (Chicago: Quest Books, 1913).

2. *Holon* is the Greek term describing an indivisible whole, within which anything affecting a part affects all.

3. Ilya Prigogine's Nobel Prize–winning concept states that matter-energy structures of the universe are maintained by a flow of energy/information into and through them, and that a change in the inflow may cause the structure to dissipate/dissolve or, in certain circumstances, re-form into a new structure.

4. Morphogenetic fields are a concept from 1920s biology that explains how lifeforms take the particular shape of their species. This concept was brought into the late twentieth century by Rupert Sheldrake in the book *A New Science of Life: The Hypothesis of Morphic Resonance* (Rochester, VT: Park Street Press, 1995) as part of his Theory of Morphic Resonance, a possible explanation for why similar events happen around the world at about the same time.

LESSON 6

1. Philippus Aureolus Paracelsus (1493–1541), born Theophrastus Bombastus von Hohenheim, was a Swiss-born alchemist and physician whose books were standard medical texts for centuries.

2. Confucius [K'ung Fu-tzu]—Chinese philosopher [551–479 BCE]; author of the Analects, one of the six Chinese classics carved upon stone between 175–183 CE, a compilation of exhortations to high moral living.

3. Though she later disclaimed his work, Eddy, during a previous marriage, when she was Mrs. Patterson, often spoke on "Dr. Quimby's Science of Mental Healing" in the years prior to his death and her writing of *Science and Health*, as documented in Charles Haden, *Spirits in Rebellion: The Rise and Development of New Thought* (Dallas: Southern Methodist University Press, 1963). For more information about Quimby, see Horatio Dresser, ed., *The Quimby Manuscripts* (New York, Julian Press, 1961); or Ruth L. Miller, *Power of Mind: Phineas Parkhurst Quimby* (Beaverton, OR: WiseWoman Press, 2011).

4. Aristides (530–468 BC), "the Just": Athenian statesman during Socrates's lifetime.

5. "Kena Upanishad," *The Wisdom of the Hindu Mystics: The Upanishads*, trans. Swami Prabhavananda and Frederick Manchester (Los Angeles: The Vedanta Society of Southern California, 1957).

6. Bhagavad Gita 8:7 (Sivananda trans.).

7. Matthew 6:33 (NIV).

8. Bhagavad Gita 9:30 (Sivananda trans.).

9. Hosea 14:2 (NIV).

10. Charles Fillmore was one of the founders of Unity and was an early student of Emma's. He spent a year "keeping an appointment with God" by just listening and, though he heard no voice, found his life transformed in the process. As a result, he encouraged the same practice for his students. For more information about the Fillmores, see James Dillet Freeman, *The Story of Unity*, rev. ed. (Unity Village, MO: Unity School of Christianity, 1978); and Ruth L. Miller, *The Power of Unity: The Amazing Discoveries of Charles Fillmore* (Portland, OR: WiseWoman Press, 2009).

11. Isaiah 1:18 (NIV).

12. Asclepius is the Greek god of healing, known in Latin as Aesculapius. He is being told by the embodiment of the Word how the universe works in this quote from a book attributed to the ancient Greek-Egyptian metaphysician Hermes Trismegistus. *The Divine Pymander* or Corpus Hermetica, Book 31:51.

LESSON 7

1. Psalms 46:10 (NIV).

2. Luke 42:22 (NIV).

3. Bhagavad Gita 10:9 (Sivananda trans.).

4. Matthew 11:29 (NIV).

5. John 16:33 (NIV).

6. Matthew 28:18 (NIV).

7. Genesis 1:24 (NIV).
8. Masaru Emoto, *The Message from Water* (Carlsbad, CA: Hay House, 2009); and Masaru Emoto, *Hidden Messages in Water* (Hillsboro, OR: Beyond Words, 2004).
9. John, 2 (NIV).
10. Eckhart Tolle, in his introduction to *The Power of Now* (Novato, CA: New World Library, 1999).
11. Proverbs 12:18 (NIV).
12. 1 Corinthians 2:3 (NIV).
13. Annie Besant, *An Introduction to Yoga: Four Lectures Delivered at the 32nd Anniversary of the Theosophical Society* (Chicago: Quest Books, 1913).
14. Tukaram Tatya, *A Guide to Theosophy*, eBook ed. (1887; repr. Bombay: Bombay Theosophical Publication Fund); available at www.bn.com.
15. Many of Hopkins's students made it a practice to always work in twos. One would treat the client and the other would treat the practitioner.

LESSON 8

1. John 12:20 (NIV).
2. Matthew 11:21 (NIV).
3. Psalms 119:105 (NIV).
4. 2 Corinthians 3:5 (NIV).
5. Psalms 23 (NIV).
6. Matthew 6:25–34 and 10 (NIV).
7. Bhagavad Gita 10:9 (Sivananda trans.).
8. 2 Kings 6 (NIV).
9. Revelation 1:7 (NIV).
10. Job 22:28
11. Bhagavad Gita 15:15 (Sivananda trans.).
12. Ibid., 10:11.
13. Jalāl ad-Dīn Muhammad Rūmī (1207–73) is considered the great mystic poet of Persia and a primary resource for understanding the Sufi philosophy. His works have been translated into English for centuries, but the most popular current translator is Coleman Barks.
14. John 8:12 (NIV).
15. Isaiah 60:22 (NIV).
16. Swami Krishnanda, trans., "The Brihadaranyaka Upanishad," Swami Krishnanda, The Divine Life Society, http://swami-krishnananda.org/brdup/brhad _V-06.html. Hopkins most likely quoted from Helena Blavatsky's *The Secret Doctrine, Synthesis of Science, Religion, and Philosophy*, Theosophical Press.

17. Since the 1980s, the Institute of HeartMath has been discovering that this may, in fact, be the case. More and more evidence is accumulating that the heart, with its rhythms and electrical signals, "conducts the symphony" that is the workings of the body.
18. Luke 17:20 (NIV).

LESSON 9

1. Maimonides (Rabbi Moses ben Maimon) (1135–1204) is a Spanish-born Jewish philosopher who is still considered among the greatest philosophers. He wrote *The Eight Chapters of Maimonides on Ethics*.
2. From *A Guide for the Perplexed*, a three-volume set of lessons said to be written by Rabbi Moses Maimonides to a student in the late twelfth century, quoted in Alexander Wilder, *New Platonism and Alchemy: A Sketch* (New York: Weed, Parsons, 1869), 8.
3. This story is most likely autobiographical, since it describes an inner process during a time when writers only did so in the third person.
4. Ecclesiastes 12:1 (NIV).
5. Hebrews 11:15 (NIV).
6. Jalāl ad-Dīn Muhammad Rūmī, *The Essential Rumi*, trans. Coleman Barks (San Francisco: Harper, 1995), 251.
7. Ibid.

LESSON 10

1. Emanuel Swedenborg (1688–1722) was a mining engineer in Sweden who, in a series of trances, conversed with angels and became a beloved philosopher and religious writer. He inspired, among many others, Ralph Waldo Emerson and Ernest Holmes.
2. Exodus 13:14 (NIV).
3. Psalms 139:8 (NIV).
4. Jalāl ad-Dīn Muhammad Rūmī, *The Rubais of Rumi: Insane with Love*, trans. Nevit O. Ergin and Will Johnson (Rochester, VT: Inner Traditions, 2007), 23.
5. For an introduction to this form of yoga, see the works of Jon Kabat-Zinn or Herbert Benson, or use the script at the end of Robert Bruce Newman and Ruth L. Miller, *Empowered Care: Mind-Body Medicine Methods* (Medigrace/Portal Center Press, 2012).
6. John 15:13 (NIV).

7. For explanations about string theory, see superstringtheory.com. The PBS *Nova* television show also has an interesting explanation in the miniseries *The Elegant Universe*, http://www.pbs.org/wgbh/nova/physics/elegant-universe.html#elegant -universe.

8. Bhagavad Gita 18:66 (Sivananda trans.).

9. Ralph Waldo Emerson, "Nature," in *Natural Abundance: Ralph Waldo Emerson's Guide to Prosperity*, ed. Ruth L. Miller (New York: Atria Books, 2011).

10. Jalāl ad-Dīn Muhammad Rūmī, *The Rumi Collection*, ed. Kabir Helminski (Boston: Shambhala Publications, 1998), 251.

11. John 8:32 (NIV).

12. Benedictus de Spinoza, *Spinoza: Complete Works*, ed., Michael L. Morgan, trans. Samuel Shirley (Indianapolis: Hackett, 2002), 153. Benedictus (Baruch) de Spinoza was a Dutch Jew in the 1600s who was expelled from his community for heresy when he published *Ethics*, in which he used a series of propositions and proofs to describe God, humanity, and our relations.

Lesson 11

1. The basis for this teaching may be found in *The Yoga Sutras of Patanjali*, written about 650 CE as a guide for seekers. A number of translations are available but the most commonly used is by Christopher Isherwood and Swami Prabaha-vananda, Vedanta Press.

2. Columbia University Medical Center, "Brain Structure Adapts to Environmental Change," *ScienceDaily*, June 14, 2011: http://www.sciencedaily.com/releases /2011/06/110613122521.htm.

3. Ibid.

4. Isaiah 44:6, 45:5 (NIV).

5. Jalāl ad-Dīn Muhammad Rūmī, *The Essential Rumi*, trans. Coleman Barks (San Francisco: Harper, 1995), 112.

Lesson 12

1. Jalāl ad-Dīn Muhammad Rūmī, *The Essential Rumi*, trans. Coleman Barks (San Francisco: Harper, 1995), 32.

ORIGINAL TEXT

ESOTERIC PHILOSOPHY: DEEPER TEACHINGS IN SPIRITUAL SCIENCE
AS PUBLISHED IN 1925

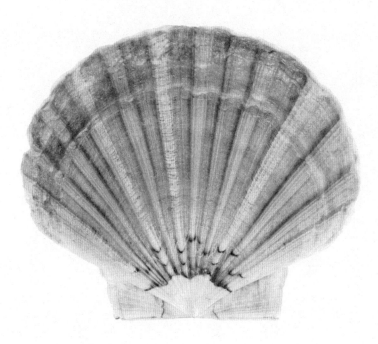

We remind ourselves of who we were in the beginning; who we are now, and who we shall be forever. I came forth from God. I know what is not God and what is God. I know now that I am God, and knowing this again, leaving all else, I am in my right Mind.

LESSON I

In metaphysics there is always what is said, and underneath what is said is what is implied. For *meta* means beyond, and beyond need have no limit. We are not limited in mental range. The ideal is able to stretch itself into the very core of things where they had their origin. Did not Boehme stretch his ideals into the Abysmal Dark, which was before even God began?

The penetrative sense of mind is its freeing sense. Without exercising its penetrative sense, mind imprisons itself in matter and sleeps. It is not content with matter. Bodies languish and enter graves because the mind has not penetrated through bodies, through things and objects, with a strong sense of things not seen. When the mind flies beyond words, when it dives below words, when it wings itself on strong pinions independent of words, it carries the molecules of bodies into light and living transfigurations.

There is a Science of sciences. It is the philosophy that mind spreads its senses over matter while words are being spoken. Hamilton, the Scotch metaphysician, called this philosophy the Science of the Absolute indifference of the ideal and the real. How indifferent to the seeming is the esoteric sense, the wordless sense and touch of mind when it lets itself loose from matter. The first lesson in the esoteric of His dogma was given by Jesus Christ in this text:

"The Lord said unto my Lord, sit Thou on My right hand till I make thine enemies thy footstool." [Psalms 110:1]

The Lord that speaks to my Lord is the Highest Brahman or Undescribed God, the First and Uncompanioned One. My Lord is my Ego or Reason. My Ego or Reason, with its sense of hearing so unlike my ears with their tympanum, hears in its own fashion, and it translates what it hears into common language. It puts what it hears from the Highest Brahman into words. It tells my tongue to speak on one side only till I see death, material limitations, misery, ignorance slip under my feet and I see myself standing upright as Jesus saying one moment in final certainty, "I have overcome the world."

The side that my tongue (the instrument of my Ego when it would sound itself on matter) must speak is that on the side where the mind is looking, there is only Good. The Good is omnipresent, omnipotent, omniscient. The Good reigns. The Good is God. The Good is Life. Life reigns on the right side where I turn my mind. The Good is Truth. Truth reigns on the right side where I turn my mind. The Good is Love. Love reigns on the right side where I turn my mind. It will sit on this side in judgment. That is my mind. It shall judge in all things, in all discussions, that the Good shall reign. And the Good shall always come off victorious. If man tells me that evil reigns, my judgment shall sit still while its tongue tells its irresistible Truth. The irresistible Truth shall ever be that the Good is there where the evil seems to be and shall reign instead of evil.

All wrong shall fail when my reasoning sits in judgment saying that because the Good is God, it cannot be overthrown. The white stone of Revelation is the Good that stays fixed eternally in the universe and reigns. Whoever sees the Good that is fixed in the universe sees the white stone. Whoever sees that the Good cannot be defeated will have it revealed unto him that even while he is thus seeing the undefeatableness of the Good, the world around him shall see it also. For his mental sense is strong, it is pungent, it is awakening. It carries even the outer senses on its wings.

Whoever sees that the Truth is God will tell the Truth, and it will defeat every lie. The Truth concerning the Good is the only Truth. The man who accuses me of wrong thoughts or wrong actions tells not the Truth. The only Truth he could speak concerning me would be of the fixed Good that is in me. If I took his purse, he shall not see theft; he shall see the fixed Good in me. So the Highest Lord tells me to see the fixed Good in my enemies, and they will have no power to hurt me. The Highest Lord tells me to see the fixed Good in the action of the thief, and that fixed Good will reveal itself even to him. He cannot help changing from thieving to kindness to his neighbors when I see the fixed Good.

The ability to sit on the right side is the ability that even the child has by native trend. The child believes in the beauty and kindness of the asp and the crocodile till it is told they are neither beautiful nor kind. The child who keeps his mind on the original idea he brought from heaven will be the Jesus Christ child.

The man who restores unto himself the idea of beauty and kindness inherent in all things will restore himself to his former glory that he had with the Father before the world appeared unto him. He has nothing to do in putting evil, matter, pain, death off the earth: he has only to sit on the right hand of all things, all people, all principle, till the Lord put all death and pain under his feet for him. Man has to insist on the fixed Good in the anarchist. He has to insist on the fixed Good in the capitalist. He thus watches the white stone of revealing. One thing after another will drop under his feet without his personal effort; yea, even without his mental effort; yea, even without his sight or feeling being touched.

"In the stone a new name: and I will give him to eat of the hidden manna." [Revelation 2:17] The promised manna of life is the unspeakable kindness of the Lord, whose undescribed presence talks in its own wondrous language to my Lord, or my talking and moving Ego, my human mind at its highest intelligence.

The first lesson to man was given many times over by Jesus, sometimes simply, sometimes abstrusely, yet always with esoteric implyings farther and farther than the ego can tell until it has sat on the side of the Good, has seen the fixed Good in all things, not with his outer eyes, not with his heart, but with his principles.

He has not spoken aloud to the poverty-stricken wretch crying with hunger; but silently, with his reasoning, he has said unto his mind, "Because the Good is God, because God the Good is kind and bountiful, thou art not hungry." This manner of secret reasoning conveys a white, fine food to the mind, which has the power to turn into bread the money to buy meat and milk for the howling wretch.

The unemployed masses must have someone to sit on the right side in principle in mind till the Good that is God takes them out of inferiority and makes them equals with kings and princes in possessions and opportunities brought forward by the steady right reasoning of some one man or woman who will not agree that their want and ignominy are reality; for the Good that is God is loving kindness and is not partial to princes and kings, leaving the poor in cold neglect.

Mary, sitting still and declaring this, shall see it everywhere. She shall convert the world. Martha, trying to make Mary see how hard life is, how slow the Good is, shall not reign. Her evil declarations shall not stand. Her estimates shall not abide. They shall fall into nothingness.

God is a providing goodness. The red of the rose is not more sure than Mary's food and beauty. So the everlasting principle of power shall reign in the sight of all men. It is the native notion of the Lord of life, health, strength, support, protection, intelligence, beauty, power, when my Lord proclaims the first lesson of Jesus in esoteric philosophy.

One of his first lessons to man was expressed in the words: "Repent, for the Kingdom of God is at hand." [Mathew 3:2] "The Kingdom of heaven is within you." "Pray unto your Father in heaven." [Luke 11:2] See how, by the philosophy of the Absolute, He here teaches man to pray unto his own Self. See how, by this lesson, He shows that the Lord, the Highest Brahman, the Father, the First One, is in all men alike. To their own God within themselves, to the highest of themselves, they shall address themselves: "Give me this day, my daily supply." [Luke 11:3] Let me not walk on the side of the hard and the unkind appearance, even when to my eyes and heart it seems so real. "Thou art my light and my life. Thou art my salvation. Great art Thou, having Thy everlasting presence even in me, ever near for me to call upon. I fear no evil, for Thou art with me."

Repentance is turning from expecting some external being to come down and do for us. Repentance is turning to the "I AM," the God, the Lord, the Father at our own center, and reasoning from its presence in us in its glory to its glory in all the earth. "Because I am, thou art." Repentance is turning from judging your life and character by the human and lying aside. It is judging it by the divine and eternal side.

The fixed Good will seem to work swiftly if I see it with my heart's conviction while I am obeying the simple direction of talking and thinking about the fixed Good, regardless of externals. He who speaks of the fixed Good is translating from the Lord's instructions into my Lord's speech.

He who sits in that judgment concerning me will behold that I am God at my center. I who hear His voice turn to behold my God. I am satisfied with myself. I am happy in myself. I behold that my own Highest Brahman is the Lord. I behold not any more human nature. Thus repenting, I take the manna of beholding God, the Lord, everywhere. To me all is God.

LESSON II

The Statement of Being, which is the title of the first lesson in meta-physics, conveys the inspiration to mind, as a wind might blow into our nostrils, that there is conflict now going on between two powers: Good and evil; Spirit and matter; Life and death; and that in the conflict, Spirit will prevail, and after the smoke of battle has cleared away, we shall see that all is Spirit, for Spirit is ever victorious when pitted against matter.

Every first lesson in metaphysics conveys this breath inward upon us. It is the inspiration or inbreathing of doctrine. But the mind is like the body in that its expiration is as important as its inspiration. The second lesson of metaphysics, or mind, is expiration. It is the throwing off or refusal of what is not vital. It is not a Truth that there is conflict between two substances, Spirit and matter, although matter is dissolved at once by presenting Spirit before it. "The earth is clean dissolved before us, saith the Lord." [Isaiah 24:19]

In heeding the injunction of Jesus Christ to sit on the right hand, we call God, Spirit. We call God, Life. We call God, Truth. We call God, Love. Thus we are seeing Life everywhere and ignoring death. We are breathing forth from our mind, its ideas not essential.

The only death there is, then, is letting go our idea of death. The idea of death is not essential to Life. There is no conflict between death and Life. The only death of hate or ignorance there can be is letting go our ideas of hate and ignorance. The idea of hate is not vital. It is not essential. The idea of ignorance is not vital. It is not essential. So, in the breath of mind outward, we let go of ideas and this is their death.

Jesus Christ said to John, "I am He that liveth and was dead, was dead and am alive forevermore." [Revelation 1:18] He spoke then of how the Jews had tried to breathe Him away from their mind; while being the vital Truth, he could not be lost but must live forevermore.

There is a presence of Jesus Christ within us, breathed through the mind by His name, which shows us that the Life that is God may quicken us into a state which has no opposite to be sent forth from our mind. There is a Life beyond the life that has to let go of death. By breathing into the nostrils the atmosphere and at the same time drawing into the mind the name Jesus Christ, we are taking in both mental and physical breaths. That name has in it a quickening energy. It expels the money changers or our sordid notions by its mystic body, which is now within us when we inspire it.

There is a life that knows no death. It is the Jesus Christ Life. The mystery of it is the state it brings us into by breathing the name "Jesus Christ," "The Holy Spirit whom the Father will send in My Name."

There is an intelligence that knows no ignorance. It is that Intelligence we breathe into our mind by drawing into it the mystic Body of Jesus Christ by the Name.

There is a Love that is beyond letting go of hate. It is the Love which inspires those who inspire, as a breath, the Name Jesus Christ. "Your joy no man taketh from you."

The Statement of Being, or first lesson in Good as Mind, as Intelligence, tells us of Omnipresent, Omnipotent, Omniscient Life. It asks us to read from the page of our own idea of Good in Life and say that there is no death in our idea of Good. It asks us to read from the page of our idea of Substance and say that it must be unfailing Presence.

It is a Science which casts out evil, matter, sickness, death, hate, error, sin. It is a Science of establishing the Kingdom of Spirit by proclaiming that all is Spirit, there is no matter; all is Life, there is no death. It is a Science which never feels the inspiration of conflict. Whereas, there is a Science of expiration of the breath of conflict. It is the Science of death, "I am He that was dead." It is the Substance which enters the body when mind breathes in the Name Jesus Christ. Ideas of death are gone. Ideas of ignorance are gone.

What were they? They were Jesus Christ in an esoteric sense. Who is the death of our former body and former mind so absolutely as He whose Name puts mind and body both out of consciousness forever and occupies them Himself? Who is so wise as He who knows a state untouched by evil and Good? This is Jesus Christ.

Our very ideas of ignorance and death are Jesus Christ. The Science of denials leads us to see that when we say there is no evil, all is Good, we are putting out Jesus Christ and retaining Jesus Christ. For the evil which we refuse is, in its esoteric or mystic sense, the ministry of destruction. There is no destroyer like Jesus Christ. "I came not to bring peace on earth, but a sword." [Matthew 10:34]

But it is not vital, it is not essential, to look upon evil and death as Good. It is vital still to say they do not exist. It is vital to say that there is no conflict between Spirit and matter, for Spirit is all when speaking of these two. For in Christian preaching, we sit on the side of Spirit and Life. Yet Jesus Christ said, "Blessed are the poor in Spirit, for theirs is the Kingdom." [Matthew 5:3] He saw that in Himself there were no pairs of opposites. He saw that Himself once being breathed into your body and mind through inspiring His Name, you would, like Him, see with your mystic body that Spirit, being one of a pair of opposites, is now melted and gone like its opposite, matter.

It is utter poverty of Spirit to be as free from Spirit as from matter. He called it blessedness. It is constant preaching of all is Good, there is no evil, which brings Good into view as the victorious, in metaphysics. It is constant preaching of all is Spirit, there is no matter, which brings Spirit into view as the victorious doctrine, in metaphysics. It there stops, and Jesus Christ takes the reins of mind exactly as promised, "I will make thine enemies thy footstool." [Psalms 110:1]

It is the "I" at the center which is exposed by breathing in the doctrine of all is Good and breathing out the doctrine that there is no evil.

Both statements are true. One swings the curtain of human experience to the right from the center, the other parts it to the left. There stands the exposed center. One breathes the breath of Truth inward, and the other breathes it outward.

The one who breathes the statements is ever independent of them all. Is not the man more important than his breath? Set free from his breaths, is he not something which is neither inspiration nor expiration?

That which is independent is the state of mind exactly identified or identical with the One who can lay down His breath and take it up again at will. What name stands for that Being? So then, he who can lay down his breaths and pick them up again at will is the Jesus Christ man.

Physically, we are told that the breath is the life of man. By the knowledge of the Jesus Christ body through Spiritual Science, we perceive that there is a Life independent of the physical. It is the metaphysical. On this point, Jesus Christ says, "The flesh profiteth nothing. My words are Spirit and Life." [John 6:63]

Then further, the words of mind which Jesus Christ and all the prophets [being, as you understand, twelve in number] taught cause you—when you use them—to be independent of words.

When we see how our true body, or our true "I," standing back and breathing in the names of God and describing His place, power and wisdom, and breathing outward the rejection of all that is not God, is, after all, only using words exactly as it uses breaths, we realize that indeed something is more wonderful than words.

What is it? It is the "I" that uses them. Here we say with Jesus Christ, this "I" is the Father or First Mover of the breath of the physical body as air, and the breath of mind as words or ideas. The "I" fathers all things, that is, it starts all things. It is the mystic body of all men alike. Whoever gets back of breaths and back of thoughts to his majestic starting point is one with Jesus Christ indeed. He knows that he is himself and God in one. Yet he is neither life nor death.

As the state which is not life, but which causes life, we see that we may also be the cause of death. "I can lay down my body and I can take it up again," [John 10:17] said Jesus Christ, referring to His handling of His outward garment of man and His hidden garment of mind.

Laying down the book you are reading seems to destroy information. Taking it up seems to revive its information. If the body that is sustained by inspiration and expiration of wind is but an appearance, is it not easy to lay it off for Him who stands back folding it around Himself? If the body, more metaphysical, which we call the mind, is but an appearance sustained by the wind of thoughts that come and go, is it not easy for the One that stands back and wraps the mind around Himself to lay it off and pick it up again?

The statement that Jesus Christ is the evil that we say has no reality, is sometimes called the only difficult statement.

Do you think it difficult to say that Jesus Christ or the "I" back of your mind must be that which stops the breath and sets it going again? Do you think it difficult to say that the "I" that stands back must be the one who stops thoughts and sets them going? When a breath stops breathing, we call it death. It is certainly the "I" back of the breath that stopped it. If we breathe inward the Name Jesus Christ and hold the breath and then let it go, we find at the fountain-head of our being a body not mixed up with the breath at all.

All the evil sights and sounds of our daily observation are the stopping of thoughts by our own "I." Let the thoughts go freely forth again and see what a change of appearance will result. Suppose a man strikes a horse. It is the "I" of yourself stopping the thought of peace. Let the thought go free again and see how peaceful the horse will feel, how peaceful the man will feel, how still the whip will lie.

Do you wonder that in the doctrine of Christian Mental Practice we have the reasonable idea that there is no pain, no discord? The simple denial of pain and discord is Truth. The understanding that the mystic "I" back of all thoughts stops them and starts them, explains why there is no pain, no discord. This "I" is again fed at its own fountain-head by its own Lord, and when we keep to the doctrine that all is Good, there is no evil, we are touching the "I" at our center, who breathes and thinks. We hear our own "I" or self taking its breath of inspiration from its Lord.

The Brahmins taught that only the "Self" can know the "Self." The words of Jesus were, "The Lord saith unto my Lord, 'Who is "The Lord?"'" It is the Absolute Self who feeds "my Lord." Who is "my Lord"? It is the "I" at my center who breathes and thinks but is always something independent of breaths and ideas. The "I" at my center is my "Self." That which the Brahmins said this "Self" might become acquainted with is its "Self" upon whom it depends, upon whom it feeds. When the independent "I" sits on the right of its "Lord," it says, "All is God." It says, "That which is not God does not exist."

Nourished by these two breaths, the religions of all ages have declared that man shall live as God forever. He may lay off his life forever. He may "rest from his labors of thoughts and his works shall follow him."

Whoever sees God sees his own "Self." Whoever sees God is God. Whoever sees God performs the works of God. Wherever he breathes his breaths, Good appears. Wherever he thinks his thoughts, Good appears. He knows that whatsoever seems evil is only his breath drawn inward. Letting his breath go free again, peace and joy and light and life are shed forth on its wings.

He knows that whatsoever seems evil is only his thoughts gathering in upon himself. Letting them go again freely, over the earth, he sees light, joy, peace, intelligence shedding themselves on their wings. He sees that he is Lord over all the earth. He sees that the denials of Science have a reason for themselves in the fact that he is as the "I" at the center is that God who breathes into the creature's breath of life, or withdraws breath—at free choice. Looking toward his God transcending himself, he sees only God and he never sees less than God.

Lesson III

"There shall be no more caterpillar" is prophesied for the days when man has embodied himself by eating his own substance. Why is there such an appearance of hunger everywhere? Is not everything longing and gnawing to fill itself with something different from what it has already on hand? This is its caterpillar state. It must ever be gnawing till it strikes its native body. Can anyone suppose that the Almighty God is gnawing after more food than He already has? So if my body is gnawing to make more substance for itself, then both my mind and my body are in the caterpillar condition, and the day of God is not known to me even though I am preaching great doctrine and making myself famous for great knowledge of God.

The eating practice of the body is called "feeding." The eating practice of the mind is called "affirmation." Both affirmation and feeding are wholly ungodly. The Lord sits in the heavens and laughs afar out of the reach of the calamities that come from eating. And the day when I cease from affirmation, that day I am the Lord and I am far out of the reach of calamity to mind. And that day when my body ceases from eating, the body of the Lord is presented alone.

"I will restore to you the years that the caterpillar [locusts] hath eaten," saith the Lord. [Joel 2:25] This is the fact. I lose no time by eating,

I lose no time by thinking, I lose no Lordship by feeding a body of flesh though I should spend a million years feeding myself. I lose no Godhead by thinking and thinking, though I should spend a million years thinking. For the years which the caterpillar hath eaten are suddenly restored, no matter what I have done or said or thought. Restoration cannot take place where something is lost. The very word "restoration" shows that the something was always somewhere to be laid hold of. So nothing is ever lost, nothing is ever gained, in fact. He who lives in fact said plainly, "Nothing can be added to, or taken from, the "I." Therefore, nothing said against any man gives him any hurt. Nothing said for a man, gives him any good. He is what he is; he always was what he is; He always will be what he is. This is Almighty God, untouchable, unhinderable.

If the world of matter fights, it is fighting for this God. So God is the innocent cause of all the fighting. Man gnaws to be satisfied and undestroyable, like the Almighty "I," but as the Almighty "I" never gnaws to get Himself undestroyable, it is plain that gnawing by fighting will not find the satisfied "I" any more than gnawing by eating or affirming.

The wisest of mankind have believed that in rest of some sort they should be satisfied. They have known that pure rest is pure God. Yet they have still kept on urging their minds and bodies to do things to find God. Their very rest has been self-torturing. Their very principle of thoughts has been self-tormenting, and as all torturing has been caterpillar effort, it is plain that man's rest is not God's rest till there is no torturing about it.

Solomon proclaimed that there never had been anything new and there never would be anything new. This is Truth. That which is already is all there is of us. We cannot change in fact. The Lord restores what we have supposed we had lost and, lo, it is now as it already was. In the various sciences, men are gnawing to discover that which already exists and work it over into combinations which already exist somewhere. In the Science of Christ, we are laying hold upon life which already exists in essence and in manifest. We say that man has all the life there is. We lay hold upon a health which already exists and we say that man already owns all the health there is. We say we lay hold upon strength which already exists, and we say man already owns all the strength there is.

Then to be seeking life, health, strength, peace, is to be gnawing after what we already have. "The press is full, the vats overflow," said Joel. [Joel 3:13] It is reasonable to conclude that if all that man is seeking is already in his possession, he would better stop seeking and rest in ownership.

In the Scriptures, the Name of the "I AM" is synonymous with His presence—and power. "Thy Name is an ointment poured forth." [Song of Solomon 1:3] "The Name of the Lord is a strong tower." [Proverbs 16:10] Do we know anyone with the pronunciation of the Lord on his lips so that the ointments are poured forth on him? Do we know anyone already showing forth that he is a strong tower? How the children shouted hosannas to Jesus because He knew the Name of the Lord. They never sang about His feeding the hungry or healing the sick. The Name of the Lord is in every man. He need not go seeking after it. Every man is entrenched in an unscalable tower of eternal safety, who owns a name that saves.

Many years ago in India lived a man whose name spoken by anyone in danger would save him promptly. Soon his name lost its safety. The Name of the Lord is eternal ointment, eternal safety. No man can tell that Name, for telling it supposes hunger to do something. So man keeps the saving Name of the Lord unspoken, untold, unthought. He keeps it where he is not hungry. Let not man suppose that by feeding his body with sufferings he shall find the unhungry Lord-Name which he already owns.

Simeon of Antioch perched on one tower 60 feet high for 37 years. An iron chain about his neck caused his forehead to touch his feet. His caterpillar nature hungered for suffering to appease its deeper hunger. As this amount of suffering did not satisfy, he added further tortures. He took only two meals per week. This is asceticism of body trying to find the "I" which needs nothing. It does not spiritualize this caterpillar per-formance to call it hatha yoga philosophy. It has been practiced thousands of years without adding to the knowledge and power of the ever-satisfied unhungry God.

When a man talks of certain actions which he must not perform and of certain actions which he must perform, he is a hungering caterpillar seeking God by hatha yoga.

When a man tells of certain thoughts which he must spin around and of certain ones which he must never think, he is a caterpillar on the mental plane, hungering after his unhungry "I" by gnawing thoughts. He does not make this gnawing more divine by calling it raja yoga philosophy. Yet one thing is done with the hungry body feeding it, viz., it is worn out; and one thing is done with the hungry mind also, viz., it is worn out with the excitement of thoughts; therefore, both mind and body are temporal, unreal, while the majestic Original Me is eternal Substance.

The Original Me, the eternal "I" Substance," is by itself, not identified with anything, yet is the eternal cause of all, as the sun is the cause of the grass, yet is never identified with the grass. As the grass looks toward the sun, it becomes more and more beautiful as grass till it finally is lost in sunshine.

The body and mind with their hungry gnawings turn to look at the divine Me, and it shines so wondrously through them that they are beautiful. They turn even to transfiguration. The look of the body toward the Original Me beautifies it. There is a power of the very eyeballs to turn up and back, which is transfiguring. There is a way of inner eyesight, the mind's eye turning backward and upward toward the Original Me, till it never has to speak or think for itself, for the original unhungry, shining Me streams in radiance through it till there is no mind whatever.

"The Lord is not slack concerning His promises," said Peter. [2 Peter 3:9] This is true, for the moment we turn the hungry eyeballs toward the throne, the Lamb that sits thereon leads and feeds with himself in the fullness of glory, so that there is no hungry body left. The inflow of the Lamb glory is instantaneous, as when a pent-up fire rushes through a draught, or as when the focused sun rays kindle on a pine board.

"Look unto Me and be ye saved, all the ends of the earth." [Isaiah 45:22] The mind's eye can turn to that Lamb on the throne with the Name that cannot be spoken. Suddenly, down through that open door, the unspeakable glory descends, and the unhungry God fills the house.

The inspiration of the Lamb is its own fiery nature. The earth that gnaws shall be filled with that nature, that glory, that inspiration. It is not by gnawing and eating, but by turning and looking.

The most heavily weighted mind may turn and look. All its weights are gone; all the Lamb's inspiration wings its splendor through it. Rahab was a harlot, but she knew her own divinity once and it so beautified her enemies that she called them divine. So they befriended her and she gave birth after a few generations to Jesus, the inspired. The cripple at the gate had seen his own Lamb on his own throne, his Original Me, and then Peter and John looked omnipotent in his eyes.

"For what thou seest, man,

That, too, become thou must;

And around about thy life,

The way be God, or dust."

The hunger of the eyes to see is sign of there being something to see, which, being seen, is all that remains. The hunger of the ears to hear is sign of there being something to hear, which being heard, that is all that there is of us. The hunger of the hands to touch and the tongue to taste is sign of there being an Original Me to touch and taste, and, when they have thus tasted, there is nothing of them but It.

Back of all the hungry senses is their Substance.

They make themselves open doors wide as God, and those doors can be no more shut forever.

Turn ye—turn ye—why play the caterpillar when the Almighty God is bread!

LESSON IV

The Adam man names good and evil. The Joshua man names good only. The Christ man names neither good nor evil.

The Adam man speaks from common sense and with fair reasoning from the merits of the question of easy and difficult, sick and well. The Joshua man finds only grapes of Eschol on the plains where Adam shows you plainly that giants of terror abide with menacing fronts. The Christ man ignores the grapes of Eschol and the giants of difficulty. He knows that good and evil are only clothes which man may put on or leave off. This is Jesus Christ in truth, namely, that which is in the world but not of it.

While I am sleeping I am in the midst of my mystic garment; but am I the garment we call sleep? While I dream, am I not aware forever that all that happens, happens unto me and I am never that which happens? If it seems close, do I not still feel that, though in the dream, I am not of it?

What is this me that is never anything that happens? What is this which is able to leave the panorama of every transaction behind me and draw it aside from me, no matter how much attention I have given it? Does my attention unto a thing make me that thing? Plato says, "That thou seest, that thou beest," but every man, woman, and child in the universe knows that he is not that which he sees. Everyone knows that what he sees is something folded around him and is no more himself than the sun was the woman that John, the Revelator, saw. When Charcot whispers to me that an onion is an orange, what is that of me which agrees with Charcot and what is that of me which sits in a serene independence of Charcot? What is the Me?

All lessons of metaphysics drive to one and one only. Notice those denials and affirmations we have gathered from the thoughts of Christian Science found in Science and Health and repeated from the books of the sages of all ages. They are every one calculated to draw us more and more closely to inquiry into who and what the body of knowledge beyond knowledge may be. If I tell of the ascetics of bygone times struggling to see this unnamed and unmoved self, I am telling of their experiments that I may avoid their unprofitable ones and experience whatever they tell in their books they have discovered that is able to clothe and unclothe them, of that which is not their Self.

Perhaps the whole metaphysics of all times might be driven down to the operation of clothing and unclothing that unseen Self. It is evident that no mystic of mighty doctrine ever did any more than wrap himself with new experiences which he called soul or mind or Spirit sensations. Is not a man something free and superior to his senses? Am I not superior to my clothes? Even if I make my clothes my chief in life, I care more for myself than I do for my clothes, for it is for myself I clothe myself. Therefore, the sages of China, of Arabia, of India, of Egypt were yet superior to and different from their experiences of Soul.

The doctrine of concentrating the mind upon concealed objects till they expose themselves has so far exposed only the clothes of the soul where men have looked toward the soul itself. And no man is ready yet to say that soul is the final body he is looking for. No one is ready yet to say that it is the Self of himself he is seeking. The Brahmins taught that it was the Self that never grows old or changes, the one that never thinks or desires, the one that never heard of loving, the Being that never heard or spoke of truth that they were seeking.

One might finally ask what is all the good, or what is any part of the good, of man seeking for the self that never ages or decays? You know that it is the push of every creature to find the best. The best is that which is free and in bliss. The push of creation is the orbit it is traveling. As the stars move on to their points in the heavens, so creation moves on to its bliss.

The operations of nature are the clothing of man's will. The operations of destiny are the clothing of his mind. The experiences of freedom from nature and destiny are the clothing of his soul. And his soul folds him around with its still more profound mystery.

When the will has confidence in itself, it finds all nature meek. When mind has confidence in itself, it finds destiny meek. When soul has confidence in itself, it is free from nature and destiny. It has no use for nature's obedience any more than Socrates may have for your rings or gold buttons. The meekness of nature and destiny is not an interesting topic of the Soul.

Understanding that—Soul, Mind, Spirit, Will, are all names used by metaphysicians to express their estimate of the being whose presence we call the Self.

When one calls God by the name Soul, he is full of loving kindness and warmth. To that one, God is life. When a metaphysician speaks of God as Spirit, he is free and unburdened. To him, God is freedom from the clothing we call flesh. When one calls God, Mind, or Intelligence, he is clothed with knowledge. We are astonished at his right knowledge. His memory, his understanding, his judgment spring forth through every movement, word, look. When one calls God Substance, there is a substantial quality about his character, his possessions, his words. When one calls God Omnipresence, he is fitting himself to diffuse and spread himself through the Universe. When one calls God Omnipotence, he feels his own powerfulness. When one calls God Omniscience, he shows forth a great wisdom.

The wonderfulness of describing God is that man becomes visibly what he has described. A confidence in himself as actually being all that he describes comes to him. This confidence is called faith. The brother of Jesus Christ called faith a healing quality of mind. "Faith shall save the sick." [James 5:15]

In simple Science, Mind, Will, Soul, Spirit are one God, and thus all confidence of the will is called confidence of God, all confidence of mind, soul, is confidence of God.

With this simple Science continually in mind for a starting point, a working efficiency of mind is recognized. It is great joy to mind to discover that it compels nature, destiny, body, and action of every kind by its own thoughts. For the practical purposes of life we might deal only with mind and its thoughts and by simple contemplation compel everything to obey our decrees. As Eliphaz, quoting from the law well known to mystics, says: "Thou shalt decree a thing and it shall be established unto thee." [Job 22:28]

But in dealing steadily with mind, we arrive at sight of another intelligence superior to mind. We grant that superior intelligence the entire right of way. We gladly call the mind which we used in making decrees a non-est claim. The writers of the books of both the Old and New Testaments are all for the most part dealing with this mind of ours which has the ability to handle material things without appearing to touch them.

When you pray for your friend to be cured, you are using your mind. At a certain point of experience in praying, you have confidence that your friend will be cured. This confidence is a living, bracing tonic in the atmosphere. He receives it and revives. If we then undertake to explain the state of mind that cures the sick, we declare that it is faith. But if the friend were looked upon in the first place as never sick, then we would not have had to rise up faith. Our faith by which we declare we cured our friend may be found at last to be only our mind opening itself to see our friend in his right state.

What is his right state? His state of reality. Have you never heard of people agonizing in prayer till they saw that it was useless to go any further, for they saw that their friend would never get well this side of the grave? Do you think they saw the reality of that friend's life? Was it not rather that they saw the limit of their own mind and did not spring beyond it? We have now agreed as a Christian people that the Jesus Christ power in man is his power to raise the dead. Jesus found that the prayer of the righteous man would prevail over disease and misfortune. But disease and misfortune are not there to prevail over. What is it that makes disease and misfortune? It is mind. Mind has a substance within itself out of which it forms its body which it calls flesh. Mind has a power to annul its own formulations with which it has clothed itself. All the mind needs to do to unformulate its clothing is to rouse its confidence.

Spiritual Science means looking at mind's native possibilities and at mind's abilities. It also means looking to see what mind is.

When a man is sick, his mind causes the sickness. When you saw him sick, your mind saw his mind's opinion. If you rally your confidence to strike off the chains of his sickness, you are only engaging in a mental fight with him. That one of you who is strongest will win.

But who is That standing back of you both that never sees chains? Does That Being know anything at all? Does the mind that is capable of talking about sickness resemble the Intelligence that never knows sickness?

So the divisions of mind into mortal and immortal have been made. The mortal mind sees and talks of sickness through its instruments, the tongue and eyes. It formulates all deformities, all ugliness. It sometimes formulates beautiful objects. But it is never the central fire. It is never the Mind that formulates nothing, which like an unnamed, undescribed splendor stands back of mortal mind and shines through its chains. Simple Science calls this intelligence which does no manufacturing of human conditions by the terms "Immortal Mind," "Immortal Will," "Immortal Spirit," "Immortal God."

It is called true faith when mortal mind does not do anything. Mortal mind parts itself. The less it knows, the less it speaks, the less it acts, the more visible does immortal mind seem to us.

All treatments in mental healing are the struggles of mortal mind to be absent. All faith is the confidence of mortal mind in itself or in what is real but out of sight. That which manufactures prosperity is mortal mind. For I say unto you that the immortal mind knows neither poverty nor riches, though it knows that these words are a winding sheet of ugliness or beauty to mortal mind. That which causes prosperity is called God. But the God that causes prosperity is mortal mind speaking of the true God who would not be immaculate if He caused prosperity.

The immaculate God knows no opposites.

When mortal mind stretches itself to win a cure of poverty and feels that it will never win the cure, we may see that its confidence in the God that is looking through it is wholly oblivious of the poverty is not roused at all.

The whole aim of metaphysics so far as faith and works are in any way concerned is to rouse confidence to the pitch of breaking open mortal mind for Immortal Mind to gleam through. The new charms of life are exposed. Even the formulations of mortal mind catch new beauties.

The Chinese sage whom they revere is the one who kept himself always at the age of sixteen years by never letting his mortal mind speak. He taught that the wise man, instead of aiming to acquire knowledge, should avoid knowledge. Not to act is the source of all power. He saw how full of formulating power the thoughts of the mortal mind are, while in the immortal mind all is finished and nothing has to be made.

Moses caught sight of this when he said that all things were created perfect and were already, before they appeared upon the earth. The fourth lesson of Spiritual Science shows that Moses was speaking of. The Mind that is not identified with flesh and blood and is not identified with the mind that forms them.

That which said, "Let there be," was superior to that which obeyed, and that which obeyed was the outer world. Its whole nature is obedience. But it was mortal mind that was used as the tongue and actor. The language that was used shows that it was the movement of mortal mind itself to stand aside for Immortal Mind to shine through.

"Let there be a firm mind" is the command to a shifting, changing, fleeting set of thoughts to part themselves and let another mind be clearly seen. It was the command which we now often make to our own mind to be still that God may be all. Whoever does this, in reality, finds that firm mind, that changeless undeviating God he is seeking. He gets the result of obeying himself. Then all things are well with him. He finds his very body permeated and diffused with that firm mind. It is the all to him. We experience this in a lesser or greater degree and call it faith. In a lesser degree, we may even say that we have confidence that great good is coming to us. In another degree, we are independent of good or ill. That which is entirely independent of good or ill is the true God. When one rises to the intensity of saying, "Thy will be done," instead of holding his own will so violently, he has risen to faith. The curtains of his mortal mind part and fade for the mighty Will of the Immortal Mind to be made visible on his pathway. There is no word for this Will. It has taken the place of the will that speaks.

It is the providence of Spiritual Science to make mind know the modus operandi of its own departure that that which is real may be realized. There are not among us any who have yet taught their mind to draw its own curtains aside and cause itself to vanish utterly. The religions of the world have not yet been understood so that the freedom men seek has been demonstrated in them. They have found mortal mind entrenched as a determined Master. But mortal mind is nothing. It is unreality. It seems to itself to be something strong and mighty, but is entirely unseen by the divine fire of intelligence that is the true God in and through all.

It is the mortal mind men have been calling God; but it never was God and never can be God. He who watches this truth is promised the absolute freedom from human experiences which religion is expected to bring. It is not our construction but our quickening and illumination which we are taught by our own soul life to expect by mental changes. Religion shows mental changes.

"We shall not all die; but we shall all be changed," [1 Corinthians 15:51] said Paul. But Paul had to step on into the next sphere without this demonstration of religious freedom.

"Be ye transformed by the renewing of your mind." [Romans 12:2] This transformation we call faith. It is clear sight of the firm mind of the one indestructible God.

There are the remnants of ten great religious systems on the earth, all having their descriptions of God nearly identical. They describe the unchangeable, firm, eternal Mind which our mortal mind falters at the sight of. In addition to Christianity, they are:

Egyptian worship;

the Hindu faiths of India, which are Brahaminism polished, refined and irresistible; and

Buddhism, a later form of Brahaminism more given to demonstrations of healing, raising the dead, hypnotic exercise, and feats of formulating and unformulating matter;

the Hebrew religion;

the Arabian religion, which is [Islam, the followers of] Mohammed;

the two Chinese religions, Taoism, and the doctrine of Confucius;

the religion of Persia, Zoroastrianism [or Parsi]; and

the philosophical systems of Socrates, Plato and Aristotle.

They all describe the mortal mind, which is the semblance and claim of intelligence without origin and without substance. They tell us that we must stand aside in the battle of life and let the warrior within us fight all our battles. This "WE" that is to stand aside, they call the ego, sometimes the lord of life, and sometimes carnal man. Our Scriptures call it carnal man. The early Spiritual Scientists call it mortal mind. Often when men speak of God, they mean the ego of man or the lord of his life, that which rules him. Thus they describe a changeable, arbitrary task master. To describe and look toward such a being is to forget how to rouse the mind to part itself for the firmament to be exposed.

Thus, Jesus Christ asked, "When the Son of man cometh shall He find faith on the earth?" [Luke 18:8]

The prevalent description of mortal mind with its unreliable kindness and its perverse cruelties has caused mind to stop far short of opening its two-leaved gate for the firm Mind of the changeless God, whose Name is beyond God, to have all things in His keeping.

The affirmations of Spiritual Science quicken and hasten mind toward giving up all that it claims to see, for that which it does not see to have the field. Paul said, "Faith is the substance of things hoped for, the evidence of things not seen." [Hebrews 11:1]

All these religions, which are now found to have been the background of Spiritual Science, described faith as that firm quality of mind which stands and sees what to all sensation and to all appearances from history and circumstances is impossible. It is the fruit which throws the husks aside. The higher our affirmations, the more faith we have, for the wider open mortal mind divides itself like the husks of the berry.

"Let there be a firm mind in the midst of the waters." [Genesis 1:6]

The Hindus practicing Buddhism strive by lofty feelings to burst the bounds and escape from themselves. They call all mind, all will, all destiny and human conditions "clothing," "robes," "bounds," "bands." They seek freedom from these things which fold them so closely that they seem to be themselves.

The Mohammedans practice denying god, by which they mean mortal mind, and affirming God, by which they mean Immortal Mind, saying, "There is no god but God."

The Brahmins deny God that they may affirm God. "From the highest state of Brahma to the lowest straw, all is delusion."

There is one Substance that stands as the body of all the robes of delusion. That is the firmament of the universe. In the metaphysics of Aristotle, this is called Energy.

The highest affirmations we can make express the most energy. They make it impossible for mortal mind to even claim to exist. In the midst of the waters of thoughts stands the unalterable One. We become nothing, for that One to be All. This is our farthest spring of thought. It exposes the One.

I am free from God that God may be God.

LESSON V

There are but twelve statements in religious science. All Bibles give the twelve. There are multitudes of ways of expressing these twelve statements. The power of the whole twelve may be in one statement. Then a Christian like Peter may convert three thousand men by one sermon. A statement of Truth is an axiom. Suppose a man says, "I am the way, the truth, and the life," he is making a statement. He may tell you that he does not believe in statements, but he is giving you one when he repeats this affirmation of Jesus Christ.

The interior life is the Jesus Christ life. Whoever shows you how to get acquainted with the Jesus Christ of you, of the ego of you merged in the divine light of the Absolute, is giving you one or two or three statements of Spiritual Science doctrine and may be indeed giving you the whole twelve.

It is excellent to be orderly in housework, it is excellent to be orderly in temple work. The mind is the temple of the ego. The ego is the "I" that thinks and talks. The "I" that thinks and talks becomes the Absolute when it talks with the Absolute. It becomes the Absolute when it thinks of the Absolute. It dissolves for the Absolute to be all in all. The light of such thinking and talking falls down straight into sight of all men. Stephen talked of heaven and of angels till even the men who were stoning him saw his face as it had been the face of an angel. It is possible to have the thoughts and speech of the mind so orderly that nothing disorderly can stay therein any more than in an orderly home.

The First Chapter of Genesis gives this order. So does the Book of Revelation by St. John.

1. The premise, There is only God. "The Word."
2. The denial of the reality of all but God.
3. The affirmation of all as Good or as God. "Salvation"
4. The faith of mind in God as Truth. "Faith"
5. The work of mind having faith in God. "Works"
6. The understanding which illuminates mind when talking and thinking of God. "Wisdom"
7. The healing of all things of belief in any other birth but the Spiritual. It is the denial of the reality of lustful passions and sensual appetites. There is no origin of creation except in Spirit. "Generation"
8. The denial of appearances of other substance end character than Spirit. The disallowance of psychology, suggestion, hypnotism, magnetic, or mesmeric influences. There is but one influence, one informer, and that is God. There is no deception. "Light"
9. The disannulment of sin. The rejection of the idea of sin. As God is all, there can be no sin. "Holiness"
10. The true creation must be manifest. It discusses the exposure of health through the chemicalization of seeming disease when truth is told to mind. "Jerusalem"
11. The disallowment of foolishness and ignorance. They are not present, The Bible denies them. "Judgment"
12. All is the perfect creation of the living God manifest everywhere. "Praise"

These twelve propositions or aphorisms of Science were all given by Jesus in His own language. They read this way:

1. God is Spirit and they that worship Him must worship Him in Spirit.

2. Ye are of your father the devil, a lie from the beginning. One is your Father, even God. Judge not according to appearance.

3. The Father and I are One. I in you.

4. Ye believe in God, believe also in Me.

5. These signs shall follow them that believe.

6. I will give you a mouth and wisdom which all your adversaries shall not be able to gainsay nor resist. God giveth not the Spirit by measure.

7. Call no man upon earth your father.

8. Ye are the light of the world.

9. I came not to condemn the world.

10. Heaven and earth shall pass away, but My Word shall not pass away.

11. Ye all know from whence I am. The Holy Ghost shall teach you all things.

12. All things that I have heard from the Father I have told you. Your joy no man taketh from you.

Many other passages go with each of these. Peter said in his first book, second chapter, fourth verse, that this doctrine that all is God is the living stone disallowed of men but chosen of God. Take it and hold the letter or proper reasoning thereof and see how the glory of God will take its seat in your system down to the foundations of your very body.

Did not Paul catch a sight of the entrance of the glorious body of Christ into his own body?

This is the esoteric philosophy or deep Spiritual Science: you have the deep glory of the interior life going on within you. So have all creatures. Science exposes it and keeps it exposed.

The twelve statements of the Bibles of the world have twelve inner glories. They are the twenty-four elders who fall down out of sight when God is exposed in His glory all over this earth.

When you or any one of you exposes the glory you had with the Father before the world, then there is nothing left on this planet that is dark or speaks of darkness.

The world will not rest a second in its present appearance when one of us appears plainly here as God, interiorly or hiddenly, as we are now God. Exposed or manifest we must be God. This is done by keeping the words of the letter of Spiritual philosophy till the Spirit claims its own.

The gate keeping each of us from this instant speaking aloud and boldly stepping forth as God in our glory, is one statement of criticism. Each prophet hid himself behind a gate of condemnation. Each priest hid himself behind a gate of caste. Each layman hid himself behind a gate of agreement with some prophet or priest. All Bibles make it clear what the gates were which hid their prophets and kings.

The deep Spiritual significance of the twelve propositions of Spiritual Science takes our attention so entirely that these gates are surely burned down. Who shall prevent our glorious God from working when we throw the searchlight of our own independent Sunshine over the universe?

The profound meditation of the Hindus for countless years has now brought us face to face with their gates of hiding and their agreement with our prophets, priests, and sages. We show them plainly our gates of hiding. They show us theirs. We show them the light of our gospel of Christ. They show us the light of their gospel of Christ. They are one light. They have the same Truth we have. There is but one Truth. Their criticisms, castes, condemnations are many. Our criticisms, castes, condemnations are legion. They are delusions. They are nothing, and as Daniel explains, "less than nought," but they seem to hide God. They are the "works of the devil," said Jesus. But the devil is a liar and the father of the liar. So a lie is the whole sum and substance of all that hides God.

The Hindus have their sages who express twelve thoughts that shall heal the world. In their philosophy, as explained by the Theosophists, we have these lessons taken from a little book of Raja Yoga in the English language, translated from the Sanskrit, as follows

Brahman is the all-pervading One.

The whole world is Atman and nothing but Atman. Atman is the Omnipresent principle.

Sitting in a solitary place being desireless, curbing passions, one should meditate upon the identification of one's self with that Atman who is One and has no distinction of place, things, and time. I am that very Brahman.

As the identity and unification of one's self and Atman is known, the belief that himself is body, senses, etc., will vanish and one will see in himself that undivided and indivisible Atman.

The meaning of Brahman is the Ever-Create. A man becomes that on which he persistently thinks.

All this universe, visible and invisible, the seer, the seen, the sight, is one eternal consciousness. The enlightened, through his mind, will be ever filled with the bliss of identifying himself with universal consciousness.

He who is free from the great bondage of desires, so difficult to avoid, is alone capable of liberation, not another, though versed in the six systems of philosophy.

Disease is never cured by pronouncing the name of medicine without taking it; so liberation is not achieved by the pronunciation of the word Brahman without direct perception. The Spirit must be sought out by intuition. Unmanifested Spiritual consciousness begins to manifest like the dawn in the pure heart and, shining like the mid-day sun, illuminates the whole universe—pure consciousness.

Deprived of the real knowledge of the Atman through being devoured by the shark of great delusions, the man becomes contemptible in conduct. The properties of pure sattva are purity, perception of the Atman within us, cheerfulness, concentration of mind on the self by which a taste of eternal bliss is obtained.

A wise man must acquire discrimination of Spirit and not Spirit in all things, as only by realizing the self in all, which is absolute Being, he becomes bliss.

Ignorance has no beginning, and this also applies to its effects; but upon the production of knowledge, ignorance, although without beginning, is entirely destroyed. The knowledge that Brahman and Atman are one and the same is true knowledge. This can only be acquired by the perfect discrimination of ego and non-ego. Ego is the

"I" that ordains and knows. The non-ego seems to ordain and know, but is nothing.

By the absence of all existence besides itself this Brahman is truth, is supreme, the only One; when the supreme truth is realized fully, nothing remains but this.

All the rest of their lessons revolve around these twelve, as all our Christ doctrines swing around twelve.

The mind of man has its "I" which ordains and moves. This is called the human ego. The Supreme God who knows only Himself, is the substance upon which the human ego relies for its movements as our shadows rely upon us for their movements. We know that our shadows have no life or substance, so the Supreme God knows that the ego of human-kind has no life or substance, and that its blessedness is its being lost in the Supreme.

Is it not the highest good of my shadow to be lost in me? Is it not the highest good of me to be God? Thus shall earthly shadows flee. Thus shall human egotisms vanish at the turn of their language toward the Absolute.

All men in supreme moments have seen that there was nothing to worship, but there was something to be. John tried to adore the angel, but the angel told him once for all he was not greater than John. Both were turning their speech and thought toward the divine truth of life in such a fashion that soon they would be dead as flesh and celestial and alive as God.

When we hear this truth, it is our business to speak forth to the schools, the churches, the business mind of the race. No matter what they say or do with us, we shall not die as majesty and strength, for majesty and strength are the unkillable breath of the Supreme Presence.

Truth was in the uncounted past and whoever told it was majestic and strong. Truth is in the living present and whoever tells it is majestic and strong. Truth will be the same in the future and whoever tells it will be majestic and strong.

Joseph had been brought up under the shadow language of talk about his youth, his limitations, his inferiority. He rose up boldly and told the sons of Bilhah and Xilpah that he was king and lord over their opinions. He told the schools and churches of the globe that his Supreme God has asserted Itself and that no man, no climate, no school, no church could be greater than His greatness. So he mastered by what seemed to be the stroke of chance but which was the natural working forth of Truth.

The Supreme Truth is that which is always supreme. Nothing can defeat it. Nothing can kill it. Its ministry is to invest me with strength, beauty, and immortality like itself. It is the stream of eternal youth, of immortal beauty, of unchanging majesty. Those who knew Truth were said in the past to stay always as 16 years of age in looks. The story of Joseph is to show that 17 years is the look of that face and figure which asserts that it is master of life and death and the commandments of men, and which knows that it is in its essence God, the Supreme.

What shall be the look of that one who perceives that the Truth is the Supreme in the sense of the Only One? What is there for this Truth to reign over? Shall that which is alone in its splendor reign over what to it has no presence? What does the Truth know of what is not Truth?

What is the body formed of Truth alone? Whose face of thought, speech, action is turned to Truth alone? How does he look? He is in our midst.

LESSON VI

Paracelsus told his neighbors that if they wished to awaken their inherent magical powers, they should continually read the book of Revelation by St. John. Magical powers are the esoteric or hidden faculties which all men possess. Confucius said that if any man would stimulate these faculties he would not need to study books. There would be an understanding of the substance contained in the books akin and superior to the mind which wrote them.

The book of St. John is a statement of a great mind directed toward our magical powers. There is a practice of directing mind toward bodily conditions and bringing out their health and beauty. This was the first claim to attention made by Mrs. Eddy's book, *Science and Health*. There is a practice of directing special attention toward the eyes of vision and causing them to see plainly; there is a practice of attending strictly to the eyes of mental understanding and drawing aside the ideas that obscure wisdom. These lessons are intended to accomplish this result. There is one for drawing out the magical powers. The book of Revelation works this miracle. It takes about an hour to read it; which was the length of time devoted by Mrs. Eddy's students to one treatment of a case that did not promptly respond. The book of Revelation is in figurative language and refers to the breaking forth of the great judgment and understanding in one mind, in all minds everywhere. Then all the powers of mind are found ours. We use them skillfully.

St. John continually addresses the inner ears of the mystic body as, "He that hath ears to hear, let him hear what the Spirit saith." Luke, the physician, in his gospel continually addresses the chord in us which is the love of God. We have one, whoever we may be, and being treated, it awakes. He calls it "Theophilus." Commentators on Luke have wondered who "Theophilus" could be. His name, meaning "love of God," tells the story.

When Mrs. Eddy wrote *Science and Health*, she brought out the principle of treatment the best it had ever been discussed. Whenever we commune with anybody or anything in any way or fashion, we treat them. We may not mean to do so, or we may mean to do so; the result is the same. The more you understand of a subject, the clearer your comrades will be on that subject. Your knowledge is a "treatment."

Aristides told Socrates that his wisdom penetrated him whenever he approached him and he felt more like the wisdom of Socrates, "Therefore, get wisdom, and with thy getting, get understanding." "They that have understanding among the people shall be wise and do exploits."

There is one Presence that we cannot elude or get absent from. It is the presence of Supreme Wisdom. It is God. If we look toward this presence continually, we look like it. We are always images of what we are looking at. The mind looks at the presence of Wisdom and shines till every part and particle of the body is transfigured. It is by the human mind or mortal mind thinking about the Divine Immortal Mind that the Divine Immortal Mind shines upon it and through it. Finally, the shine of the Immortal Mind on the mortal mind discloses the tremendous fact that there is no reality or substance or presence or claim or anything whatsoever of the mortal or human.

When a speaker is telling about mind as an instrument, he is quoting from the doctrine of the Brahmins on the mortal or the human mind. He does not mean the Great Presence whose name is Immortal, Divine Understanding. That is not an instrument. It does not speak our language, yet when we look toward it we speak a language. It does not think anything, yet when we look toward it we think thoughts. We hear speakers and we read writers and they say, "There is one Mind thinking thoughts. It is the only Mind. It is Divine, Immortal Wisdom." They mean this great Presence whose influence is so powerful upon our mind when we look toward it that we think like new creatures.

Then again, speakers and writers use the term "Ego" for both the human one in you which governs the body and the "Divine Ego," who knows nothing of the body.

You must have what the Theosophists call "discriminative knowledge" and separate promptly and without error the ego human from the Ego Divine. You must separate promptly and without error the human or mortal mind from the Divine Immortal Mind. You must separate physically visible material nature from spiritually visible Spirit. Some speakers and writers talk more of nature and intellect. Examine them closely and you perceive they are describing the unreal delusive phenomena of the physically visible world of matter. It is an interesting system, but it is not Spirit. It is what Mrs. Eddy calls the dream creation. It is what the Buddhists call maya, or delusion.

If the speaker or writer tells you that it is of delusion he is speaking, you feel the knowledge of truth spring up at once. It is a good treatment of the chord in your being, which is "the separator," as our Bible terms it; "the discriminator," as the Eastern books term it. It is the final dissolving of outside nature to know it as delusion and unreality. It is the exposure of reality and glory.

Suppose you think the substance of the quinine pill is God? It will act like a drawing to one side of curtains on the quinine pills. The power of God will stand out from it. It will have a healing effect. God is health whenever spoken of in any way or anywhere. Suppose you say that the substance of your voice, the substance of your glance of eye, the substance of your touch, is God? The power of God will be exposed by so saying. Everything you do will have a healing quality.

The very mention of God is the mention of a healing power. One name of God is Jesus Christ. It is a wonderful discloser of covered faculties to look toward the Jesus Christ in all things. The greatest miracles are wrought by looking toward the Name of the Great Presence of Wisdom.

No matter what errors you keep in your mind, you can be a miracle worker, if you look toward this mighty presence whose most miraculous Name is Jesus Christ. You may even believe that there is a devil, like Gasner, who cured all kinds of disease by applying the name Jesus Christ to the men and women as a present of irresistible health. You may call God a great Person sitting on a throne as the faith-cure workers of our own time do, who do indeed cure all manner of disease by applying the name Christ or Jesus Christ to the people as a present irresistible health.

Errors count nothing—simply nothing—while you are looking so steadily toward this almighty Presence here just before us.

The way we have of looking toward this Presence best is by talking to it. Hosea said, "Let us take with us words and go unto our God." Mary, the Mother of Jesus, did not speak. Her mind was not thinking a single thought. This gave the Wisdom now looking at us the free passage through her mind. We are able to be as free to the transit of an unprejudiced idea through us by keeping our mind facing the Divine Mind till the divine is all there is of us.

There is an instant after speaking when we do not speak. There is an instant after thinking when we do not think. This instant is the silence in heaven which Mary felt. She brought forth a Wonderful Counselor, a Mighty God, by being entirely divine. We may bring forth our own ordained works by being so lost in the sight of this Presence that we are It only.

The Arabians taught of the drawing power, the irresistibility of it, by the story of the mountain which, when a ship should sail in sight of it, would cause the craft to go all to pieces. The nails, the steel bands, the iron chains, the metal fastenings and tools would leave the ship and fly to the mountain. The wood, hay, and stubble of the ship would disappear. So we, if we sail the ship of our mind toward the mountain of God, here in our midst, by thinking and thinking of God, shall be no more human beings but transcendent, divine beings. We shall be what the genuine quality, the true substance of us, already is—God manifest.

The mind, which we have called an instrument, will be wood, hay, stubble. It will be pure nothingness. The Jesus Christ mind will be all there is of us.

The flesh as a changing, homely, hateful, even as a loveable thing, will be gone. The mind, with its errors, with its strife to be true, will be gone. Only the eternal body in its beauty, only the Divine Mind with its brilliant understanding will be left. "For we know that if our earthly house of this tabernacle were dissolved, we have a building of God, an eternal habitation."

This is what all science, all religion, all books, all philosophy, every study, are trying to expose. Understanding is the well-spring of life.

In Mrs. Eddy's book, which first introduced Christian Science as a healing principle, we find the idea that Understanding is the divine Self at work. That is, if one sits in the presence of a sick person and understands that his disease is delusion—nothing, and understands that really he is divinely whole and perfect, the patient is sure to get well at once. His divine spiritual nature comes forward and he shows good health. On this same principle, an idiotic child has a brilliant mind at the center of his being, and if any of us understand this to be true, the intelligence of that child will come forward in proportion to our understanding. David said that by understanding the heavens are formed and the earth and all things therein. Understanding is One. It is all in all as the sun is all in all of the atmosphere. Focused on the idiotic child's gross appearance, it burns it off as the focus of the sun's rays upon any object burns it off.

We learn a habit of concentrating our own understanding upon one thing or another according to what science we are studying. If we are studying the Yoga books, we shall call understanding by the term "discriminative knowledge." We shall be told upon what to focus our attentive mind—almost always upon some material thing. Then we will find the ego, or central intelligence, of that thing and it will expose certain wonderful information. For instance, we are told to concentrate our mind upon the moon and directly we will know all about the fixed stars. But pure Spiritual Science recommends fixing the mind upon the

God here present. Jesus Christ said, "Seek first the kingdom of God, and all these things will be added unto you."

It is my business to distinguish and distinguish instantly between the concentration of mind on one universal Spirit equally present everywhere and the concentration of mind on the nose or on the moon or even on a word. The Buddhists and Brahmins teach that to concentrate the mind upon such a word as "friendship" will draw friends to us as to magnets.

Jesus is the friend unto whom the world now turns, and His whole attention was fixed on the one God here present, whom to understand is to be exactly like, the same in all qualities, the same in all powers.

Though one teacher may be telling of the soul that sinneth and another may tell that the soul is sinless God, shall you be distracted? Though one may talk of a wounded spirit and another may tell of the spirit that is free from all that transpires, free to be a spectator of the great delusion of the universe or not see it, the one Free Spirit, who is the untouchable God, shall you be distracted? Though one may tell of the mind that makes mistakes today and does wisely tomorrow, while another man shall say that Mind never makes mistakes, for it is God, shall you be distracted? Though one teacher may talk of mind as if there were two minds, viz., a human mind and a Divine Mind, shall you think there are two minds? Would you say there were two boats because you saw a reflection of your boat in the water under you? Is there any human spirit in reality? Is there any mortal or deluded mind in reality? Is there any human or carnal man in reality? If I speak of one, can you tell instantly whether I speak of the unreal boat that glides under our real boat or of the boat we are sailing in? If I speak of the mind as an instrument, do you know instantly whether I am speaking of what glides along dealing with things material or of that One Intelligence from whose storehouse we draw understanding of how to handle the mind we use? If I speak of man, are you instantly cognizant of whether I am speaking of God or of an inverted image of God?

Do you know why we speak the most unbelievable and wonderful things to a world which has all its attention turned toward matter? It is because mind pulls the material things around with it. Shall you not love to seethe prophecies of the good and noble of all ages fulfilled, when, by our understanding, we have straightened up all downcast and beautified all imperfect things? This is promised to be the first signal of the understanding fire within us being focused on God, whose name is Understanding.

Do you realize that we must speak of understanding if we would understand well? Do you realize that if you want to see the fine fleet of light that streams between the small air globules that close around us, you must watch for it and think about it constantly?

Do you realize that there is one topic upon which you can fix your human mind that will erase the human mind and show the Divine Mind? Do you know what you ought to fix your grieved soul upon till your soul that is capable of grieving is lost and the soul that is above all human passions is present?

"Come and let us reason together." Let us attend to our own sunshine, our own God nature. Shall not we be the God that sets the unhappy world into peace? Shall we not be the hot fire that shall consume the dross that now covers the brightness of men and women and children?

It is by understanding our own splendor that we burn down the barriers that hide our ears from hearing the wonderful choirs that are now singing near us. It is by understanding our own hot splendor of Intelligence that we burn off the scales that hide the sight of what is going on around us.

There comes a moment when understanding springs forth in some direction.

One man's understanding heals all manner of disease wheresoever he walks. One man lets a streak of bright sunshine go free by much thought on the way of the Spirit, and wherever he walks he speaks brilliantly, originally, powerfully of God. We wonder at him. One man lets his sunshine of understanding stream through him toward the world by focusing his thoughts till they burn through unhappiness. Everybody is happy when his mind thinks of them.

Thinking of God, we are thinking of a fire that will consume everything except itself; therefore, as our walls feel the flames, we are all illuminated, inspired, on some line. We work miracles on that line. Thinking and still thinking of God, we feel the fires of His burning taking down other gates and we work other miracles. Thinking and thinking of God, we burn down still other bars, still more plastering; we work other miracles. Thinking and thinking of God we find ourselves God. We do all things. The former heaven and earth are no longer visible to us. We are the light of our world as God is the light. We are the heat of our world—as God is the heat of the universe. Thinking and thinking of God melts the rocks and the mountains. Thinking and thinking of God dissolves flesh, the glorious body of Jesus Christ which was with us before the world was, which is with us now, and which we never can get away from, is visible. We are not changing, discordant creatures. We, by thinking of God understand God. We do not have to walk among sorrowful beings. Thinking and thinking of God, we understand the God who speaks as man or as beast everywhere.

How much God intelligence has shed Itself through you now? Do you see upright, irresistible men and women and horses? Are they out of the reach of pain or hunger in your eyes? Does everyone look handsome, healthy, brilliant with wisdom in your eyes?

How long have you been making God the one theme upon which you have fed your mind? Do you eat the Name of God with your mind as you eat your breakfast? Do you eat the Name Jesus Christ with your mind as you eat your dinner? Is God all in all to you? Through and through you? Do you understand why the Name Jesus Christ is a Name that burns and cracks the plastered walls that have kept you appearing in a house of flesh and blood, skin and bone? Is it because that Name stands for one that took the human mode of thoughts and fed them on God till the understanding of God made that mind all God? It is because that Name stands for one mind that took a human appearance and ate the Name God; that loved the One Presence, that concentrated upon the one Spirit till the glorious spiritual body shone out in full sight. It is because that Name stands for one who, though drawn into the appearance, kept calling Himself God and would not be other than God for one instant. He would not forget His own Substance. He conquered by conscious knowledge of His Spiritual origin and everlasting quality. He made the earth a plaything. He handled its serpents as one that knows himself the master of serpents, through conscious acquaintance with God. He called health into sight, life into sight, through making health and life as obedient as serpents, by conscious knowledge of God, whose presence will fire you with understanding of how to handle life, health, strength, peace.

Jesus Christ is a Name that stands for one who dwells at the center and moves Life and Spirit through the Universe, or does nothing with life and Spirit, according to choice. When we turn our mind toward that Name, we are arriving at the same freedom. All men have the Jesus Christ freedom at their center. When I understand Jesus Christ through thinking of God as Jesus Christ, through meditating upon the Name as the Brahmins meditate upon One, I shall be Jesus Christ in the new Name which no human tongue speaks, which no man knows who sees anything whatsoever that hurts or discourages.

Whoever understands God through concentrating upon the Name Jesus Christ has the Holy Ghost power. Whoever understands God through concentrating all the attention of his mind upon the Name Jesus Christ remembers all that he knew with God in the beginning and can tell boldly and brilliantly all that he now knows. Concentrating the sun rays, we burn the wood, hay, stubble. Concentrating all the God seen into the Name Jesus Christ, we burn away sorrow and foolishness, matter and mind.

To understand is to believe or not believe wisely. If we understand God through concentration of mind upon the Name Jesus Christ, we do not believe in the reality of matter, we do not believe that evil or sickness can conquer. We believe that the Spirit of man will rise in unconquerable majesty if we see it in a man. We believe the Spirit will rise in him and be noble, healthy, beautiful. We see it in all men present; therefore, we believe in it and testify that we do see. And our testimony is true.

The divine Pemender saith, "These things, O Asclepius, will appear to be true if you understand them; but if thou understandest them not, incredible. For to understand is to believe; but not to believe is not to understand."

We understand God through feeding the mind on a Name. The Name rushes from center to circumference of all things now. We hold no longer on to the Name. We are the Name. We eat no more of God. We are God. We speak no longer of Jesus Christ. We are Jesus Christ. We are not human. We are divine. We are not seeking to understand. We are understanding. We are not in the world or of the world. We are all that is.

"Is there anything besides me? Nay, I know not anything." To know myself is understanding. I understand myself; therefore, I understand all there is to understand. I am all; therefore, all understand. Hath it not been written that the understanding of one is the understanding of all?

LESSON VII

After the mind is dissolved from the claim of being an instrument into the knowledge of being God, the whole world, with all its people, the whole canopy of heaven with all its stars, all things above, beneath and around, are exposed to their actuality.

It is the Adam mind that sees God and names Him animal, plant, bird, human nature. The Christ Mind sees God and has a language of his vision which the Adam mind comprehends not. Everything has a language of its own in imitation of the language of the Absolute. The wrens that chatter in the trees understand their own language. The heart beats while the head is cool and indifferent. Something addresses the heart which the eyes cannot see, as something addresses the ears which the hands cannot touch. And each of these conversations is the signal to us of the one speech of God going on all the time. Only God understands God. It is the highest speech that tongue can offer concerning the ears and their language to say that they do not hear. This leaves God alone as hearing. It is the highest speech that the tongue can tell of the language of the eyes to say that they do not see. God is the only sight. It is the highest speech the tongue can utter concerning the language of the mind to say that it does not think. This leaves the only Mind to be the Mind that is God.

"Be still and know that I am God" is the language of that Mind of which mind is the symbol. Only the language of the Absolute is a true language. It is only from knowledge of the Absolute that we can be wise.

The stillness which is enjoined upon what are called our organs of sense or our faculties, with all their peculiar tongues, is making them all plastic receptacles for the inpouring of the Absolute. Perfect stillness is entire openness. Entire openness is the reception of the All-Knowledge.

On small and imitative scales, we see this principle operated by the photographic plate which takes the contour of a large object, and also by a man's mind which becomes negative for you to imprint your whole character upon him so that he is called a character reader. For him to be entirely plastic to you would be his being lost into your being and will. Thus we have the still possibility of being entirely lost in the Absolute—which is our reasonable service, as Paul declared.

"Not my will but Thine be done," said Jesus.

You can see that no man would be so powerful as he who had resolved himself unto God. This is meekness, which is Omnipotence.

"He that is greatest among you, let him be your servant," said Jesus Christ. "I am meek and lowly of heart." "I have overcome, the world." "All power is given unto Me in heaven and in earth."

Seventhly, then, in scientific order of concentration of the Absolute, Moses said the earth should bring forth works. "Let the earth bring forth." So mind, made nothing as an instrument, becomes by such meekness, brilliant with understanding and serves like Jesus Christ. It brings forth. Water is meek to its thought or to its spoken word. It changes into wine. It will change into whatever substance you please.

The body of mankind is meek as water to one who has himself risen from entire openness to entire wisdom. Nobody can withstand your orders. You are Jesus Christ in fact. To Jesus Christ every knee shall bow. The Jesus Christ Mind is wide awake—widely open consciousness. It does no miracles accidentally. It is as thoroughly competent to do the next miracle that is presented as the first one. Why do not Christians work every miracle with prompt and equal skill? Their miracles are not the work of understanding. They are not conscious of Themselves.

The book of Genesis teaches the consciousness of Mind. To read the first chapter is to find ourselves waking up to our God Mind by loosing our hold of our mortal mind.

Conscious miracle working is consciousness of God. The miracles need not to be wrought in the estimation of one who has no mind, no life, no thought, no language, but lets whatever is, remain as it is. It is the Jesus Christ wisdom that sees God in the tree and sees no tree, sees God in the convict and sees no convict.

When that which is true is mentioned, it is exposed. This is bringing forth.

When that which has no time is mentioned, it is exposed. This is bringing forth. When that which never heard of death or life is mentioned, it is exposed. This is bringing forth. When that which never heard of mind is mentioned, it is exposed. This is bringing forth.

The language of the heart is reported by the tongue. The language of the ears is reported by the tongue. The language of the life is reported by the tongue. The language of death is reported by the tongue. Therefore, Solomon says, "Death and life are in the power of the tongue." And again, he says, "The tongue of the wise is health."

The language of that which thinks not of life or death is reported by the tongue. The language of what is absolutely changeless is reported by the tongue. The curtains of sight are closed when the tongue reports the language of the ears only. While one describes wonderful music perfectly, we do not see the music nor see the reporter. Eyesight is forgotten. The ears are deaf while a wonderful painting or a wonderful face gazes toward us. So all the senses of man, so all the mind and thought of man are still when the tongue tells skillfully the language of God or that which is and alters not. "Eye hath not seen, nor ear heard, neither hath it entered into the heart of man to conceive what God hath prepared for them that love Him."

The sage of India who showed the German traveler some old manuscript books told him that the true sage never wrote books, never talked, never made effort to teach. He had barred his mind by silencing all its operations to receive the imprint of the ever present Wisdom and whoever should come into his presence would receive what he knew in like manner or remain ignorant.

What that language is which the One-present Being is imprinting on the God-Being at our center, only the God in us knows.

Whatever is unalterable truth must stand forth. This is bringing forth. The nearer the tongue comes to telling the unalterable Truth, the more perfect the bringing forth of health, life, intelligence.

The tongue speaks the language of Omnipresence and the mind designs to extend itself to greatness thereby. But the electric spark that occupies no room is the Omnipresence of the universe. By some clash, it is exposed, and houses are burned and men destroyed. They show themselves to be at their native estate, of the same substance as the spark at its invisible presence. So that by one visibility of the Mind that is not visible to the human mind or to the eyes of man, the whole human mind with all its friendly senses is burned away to be as the spark of that Absolute that stays here and waits.

"The heavens shall roll away as a scroll. The elements shall melt with fervent heat."

We are told in the Raja Yoga philosophy of India, that the earth ego is shrouded by five sheaths which right doctrine will dissolve, and that the man ego is shrouded by five sheaths which the right doctrine will dissolve. The right doctrine is the true statement of what God is, what nature is, what man is, what life is.

In a little book of translated aphorisms by Tookeram Tatya, we read, "A wise man must acquire the discrimination of Spirit and not-Spirit, as only by realizing the Self which is Absolute being, consciousness and bliss, he himself becomes bliss."

The "I" that is conscious of the gross body and is hurt or pleased by what happens to the gross body is the human ego. So long as that which happens in the gross world is observed and changes, we are human ego, human mind. This "I" is one of the sheaths of the divine Spark. By dissolving the human "I" or ego, the shining Absolute breaks forth and the gross body disappears.

All the points of Jesus Christ doctrine are directed to the dissolving of the sheaths of the Soul Ego, or the Divine Spark, the God Self: First, by the right doctrine of the Soul, mind, nature, and matter; second, by the right doctrine of Ego, God, invisible, un-nameable One; Third, by ceasing from doctrine altogether.

Never till the tongue is speechless, the mind dissolved, the ego melted can truth be known—be exposed—be brought forth. Then all doctrine is seen to be not.

Then the "I," the Ego, the so-called God is seen to be not. Then Truth Absolute, as our language has it at its best, is seen to be not.

That which Is is not that which can be told.

There is something that is free from all union. That is which Is. That which is unattached, is free. That which is free, is God. Hence he who looks toward freedom by doctrine is looking toward God.

To look toward freedom by doctrine is to use an instrument to view the heavens or the insects of earth. Doctrine treats of omnipres-ence. This is telescopic information. Doctrine treats of the inconceivably small. This is microscopic information. Each takes the mind from its habitual tracks and shows to the senses new territories.

But no doctrine is truth. All doctrine is but an instrument to distract the mind's native knowledge from Truth. The purpose of Jesus Christ is to set mind free from doctrine, to turn it to see the Absolute, and thus, to be the Absolute.

Science teaches to ignore science. Doctrine leads to dropping doc-trine. Talk of God leads to no talk of God.

Spiritual Science leads away from science. Spiritual Science dissolves science. It dissolves itself. Its only mission is finished when we know there is nothing to say, for there is nothing to know. The Truth is unknowable by that which is dissolvable.

Truth is known only to itself.

Only God brings forth God. God is what IS.

LESSON VIII

There are three interpretations given to Scripture writings. These interpretations constitute the three great doctrines of men:

1. Literal
2. Mental
3. God

Take the words "bottomless pit" as an example. The literalists see and feel according to common sense that there must be a bottomless hole to contain all the billions of existences that have been inhabitants of the universe and will be dwellers here in the future who have trespassed and erred.

The mentalists, or those who resolve everything into mind, declare that there is no bottomless pit except in the desire of the mind. Nothing, they explain, can satisfy the mental desire. Give a man everything he asks for, and he is still a sandy plain ready to suck in something else. Desire is bottomless vacuum.

God being the only One, those who take the passages of Scripture spiritually are found declaring that the God in man swallows all that has being and all that has existence. The unlimited One is the consuming fire which swallows death and hell, heaven and paradise, being and not being. Is it not written that death and hell are swallowed up in victory? Is it not written that Jesus Christ is the victory that swallows death and hell?

Jesus Christ is a Name of God consuming the universe. "I draw all men unto Me." Is it not the word of Jesus Christ that all things are delivered unto Him of the Father? Who so glorious in peace as he who eats and contains all things and is satisfied? It is the Jesus Christ in man that calls for all things to be consumed in his own body. It is God containing God. This is illumination. This is the shining light. This is smokeless fire. This is the light of the world.

Whatever interpretation of Scripture pleases you best is your illumination such as you have. And your illumination is your doctrine. Doctrine acts as a light to the feet and a lamp shining on the pathway to be one's defense and gloriousness, or his Hades and pain. Send on ahead of yourself your proclamation of what is according to your interpretation and you will find every stone and tree moving itself either out of your way to give you free transit or into your way to hinder you when you arrive at that object your doctrine prepared for you. "My word," saith the Lord, "is a lamp unto your feet." "My word," saith Satan, "is plainly spoken by you when you realize satanic conditions."

"The letter killeth," says a bold text. That is, whoever takes the Scripture as it reads literally, must be material and go out as matter goes out, namely, in death. For we find that the letter preaches a doctrine of death; therefore, that letter being a man's highest light arranges his pathway. It is his lantern. It is the doctrine that transfigures and delights the pathway which interprets Scripture as God. He who takes the lake of fire to be a literal, material Hades must have much heat of life's battle. "In the world, ye shall have tribulation." He who finds the lake of fire a hot remorse of mind for his errors has a double torment, for thus both his mind and his body enter into daily tribulation.

Is it any advantage to think that all the blindness there is, is mental-blindness, since mental states shadow themselves on the etheric walls of creation and make bodily states?

To admit that I cannot hear the voice of the Lord will not only shut my mind to the knowledge of God but will affect my outer ears. Very likely, I will have a number of deaf people making my pathway more difficult daily; but if I tell them the Lord God is the only deafness there is, since one who contains all things cannot hear outside of himself, I find I myself am that one whom I acknowledge and what is not myself I cannot hear.

Such a doctrine turns me toward myself. It is my own word lighting my own mind. I see thereby that I may make some deaf people if I choose. I see that I may have physical deafness if I please. I perceive that I may have a world of people hearing what pleases them and deaf to what does not please them through the doctrine I hold. I see that they may hear what is not pleasing to them if I hold either the interpretations of matter or mind while I read Scriptures. My doctrine is my lamp which lights my life with splendor or lurid haze.

Only the God-interpretation can illuminate my life with what satisfies me. By this lamp I find every object and every event a subdued instrument for my use without effort on my part. My only effort has been the carrying of my doctrine as a man carries a candle.

Things are subject to doctrine. Minds are subject to doctrine. Things and mind are exposed by doctrine.

Why does a man dig in the gold mines or work shrewdly with his fellowmen to get their gold? Because it is the nature of the doctrine he believes in to compel his efforts in one of these directions.

Could he have a doctrine that would undo effort? He could. This doctrine of Jesus undoes effort of all minds. In the midst of the world of effort, the man with the doctrine of Jesus lies down and sits still while all things arrange themselves in order to please him. As the Scriptures read, "He maketh me to lie down in green pastures." "Your heavenly Father careth." "Take no thought." "Thy will now be done."

The doctrine of Jesus is the doctrine of ease. It is the doctrine that exposes things that are already formed, for it is the oldest teaching of mankind that things are already created before they appear. He who has right doctrine has a lamp that exposes what is already made; therefore, the principal thing to obtain is right doctrine.

Doctrines are the light that Moses said, "Let there be." Disturb them not. Despise them not. Let each man try his own lamp and see what is already made from the light his own doctrine throws upon it.

One man, by his own lamp, sees provisions in abundance in a city that is starving. By steadily keeping that lamp shining on that city, these abundant provisions do exhibit themselves to all the citizens, and the man with the lamp has not stirred from his chair. His doctrine reads: "Plenty for poverty"; "Beauty for ashes"; "The oil of joy for mourning."

Elisha's lamp exposed the horsemen and chariots against whom no army of men could fight. Persistently holding his lamp, his man-servant's eyes also beheld the celestial warriors. The doctrine of Jesus promises that every eye shall see and every tongue confess all that is exposed by the steady holding of the Nazarene's candle toward the universe of God.

Elisha's doctrine reads, "Legions of angels defending the good."

The doctrine of Jesus reads, "The Kingdom of God is come." There is nothing to be created—all is created. There is nothing to be done—all is done.

Your doctrine shines on what is already done and sees nothing but a mass of matter crude, but waiting to be used; or your doctrine shines on the kingdom and shows you a mass of matter and mind crude, but yielding to your orders. You have a mental training which reads, "Thou shalt decree a thing and it shall be established unto thee." So you decree. If your former doctrine read of ugly, hard labor as the lot and law of life, your new doctrine of decree is not yet your hearty doctrine. The labor lamp still sheds its lurid light on the kingdom of God.

If the "decree" doctrine still clings to your mind, the doctrine that "All is finished" is not your light. Decree sheds its electric beams on the kingdom of God at your hand. All is yet artificial, unsatisfactory.

It is easier to "let be" than to decree. And the doctrine of "let be" is the one doctrine that sheds the perfect light on the Kingdom of God here in our broad daylight of our own understanding which we had with the Father before the doctrines of men shed their candles on our mind and invited us to see the kingdom of God from other standpoints than from the light we had and which we were forever.

The letter of Scripture would make me believe that all is darkness in the world and over the world. The letter of Scripture would have me think I had not light of understanding but must get the light from God. The mental of Scripture would make me think that I must speak and think in order to be power and bring forth good.

The spiritual understanding or the God-interpretation would show me that all I have to do is to be. All I have to think is nothing. All I have to speak is nothing. That which was and is and ever will be, cannot be altered by any doctrine I may preach, but my doctrine will cause what is now to show itself as not what is desirable but as that which is heavenly peace and the kingdom that Jesus Christ saw and still sees.

We now know that the right track toward our own smokeless flame of understanding is the only repenting which God knows anything about. If my doctrine turns me toward the flame that cannot be extinguished, which never was extinguished, which will burn forever within my own being, I have repented, that is, turned toward my own God nature. By so doing, I no longer look to another for my information, my inspiration, my happiness. I find all this in myself.

It is the testimony of Jesus Christ that when a man touches right doctrine, he turns with it to look toward his own heart. He does not despise his heart as a physical thing with no reality; he looks toward it as a point of light shining forth from his whole body. He does not despise his heart as a mind center and thus only an instrument to use; he looks toward it as the One only Light. Therein he finds his original form, his first beauty, his undimmed wisdom, his pristine splendor as God. He finds that his own heart is worthy of his whole attention. It is keeping his lamp trimmed and burning for a man to look toward his own heart till he sees within it all that it contains of the God Fire. Then, from that understanding, he is able to shed a light on the heavenly kingdom nigh him which shall not fail.

Jesus Christ received no doctrines from men. He turned Him toward the light that was in Him as in all men before the world was. "I am the Light of the World," was His doctrine when He lost Himself in His own heart flame.

Men of old practiced sitting with their eyes turned toward the heart centers in their own bodies till it exposed the divine prototype of themselves as a being all-glorious. To their first gaze nothing was glorious; to their steady gaze, it became glorious. To their first gaze their own prototype seemed small; to their steady gaze it became mighty and like a devouring flame. Into it all the worlds were able to merge. As Isaiah prophesied, "A little one shall become a thousand and a small one a great nation," and in their Bible they proclaimed, "God is the smallest of the small and the greatest of the great."

As all things far away have the reputation of being small to the eye of sense, so Jesus Christ, the farthest away of all beings according to our sense, seems inconceivably small to that one who thinks of Him as within His own heart. Is not the heart regarded as a small organ performing one of many missions? But what if now the heart is found to be the chief and only organ possessed—so stupendous in its office that when man looks into it, he becomes no longer a man of flesh and bones, but the transcendent Christ? If this doctrine shines with any splendor for you, then one more turn from the literal to the spiritual has been made by you. The heart is God. It contains God.

This is a light which Moses said, "Let be." He who understands his own heart, understands God. He who looks out toward the kingdom lying here at our hand from the knowledge which is within his own heart looks from God to God. The true light then shines. He says with Jesus Christ, he says as Jesus Christ, he says it as God—"I am the Light." As God, he says, "I am Understanding." He speaks as God. "Now is come the Kingdom."

"The heart affords a great light," says the Hindu Bible. "It illuminates the senses. In it resides memory, reflection. It is the imperishable one. It is the lamp and center of the body." All Scripture is God. Interpret it as God, and see God.

All your body is God. Interpret it as God, and see it as Spirit unhindered. Nothing clings to Spirit and darkens it.

And all that you have of heart in your religion, so much understanding you have.

According to your heart, you are a seer of God or a seer of not God. Let there be light on this kingdom which lies here at hand. Let many doctrines light as best they may, but only in me can I see it plainly. Let it be plainly visible because my heart is single to one God. The pure in heart shall see it. The understanding heart shall see it. The single eye is my heart.

"The kingdom of God cometh not with observation," said Jesus, but with the knowledge that God is in me, the pure unalterable One.

Whatever doctrine men may turn as lamps on the mighty City we now dwell in the midst of, let me be not deceived into conceiving any doctrine but of the heart.

LESSON IX

Maimonides, who was wise in sacred history, said of the book of Genesis, "Whoever shall find out the true sense of the book of Genesis ought to take care not to divulge it. If a person should discover the true meaning of it by himself or by the aid of another, then he ought to be silent, or if he speak of it, he ought to speak of it but obscurely and in an enigmatical way."

Evidently, Maimonides knew that the book is a parable with a motif. It tells important Spiritual principles in figures of speech. In our day, there are many who doubt entirely that there were ever any such characters as are therein mentioned. It has been called a book written by intuitional memory.

Esdras, a Hebrew priest of 457 B.C., had the experience which mathematicians, musicians, and others have sometimes, of suddenly recollecting that what they are doing they have done before, and that there are yet other points about it that they have known. So as from one point to another, they go on making it known to the world; others call them original and wonderful, but they know that they are remembering.

A child one early morning waking tried, with mysterious steps of mind, to remember where that home was from which she had come;

but soon the sounds and sights of her earthly and familiar home caused her to forget to think of some long past spot and scene. Again, in middle life, came the same experience of trying to remember some wonderful and happy life long gone. So the profound mathematician recollects what once he has known in some other life experience.

Thus Esdras (or Ezra) touched backward upon some points of thought as he had them with the Father before the world was and told his mind's past knowledge in a story. By it, he explained how the Spiritual world is good and uncognizant of matter or evil. He sees the power and splendor of the Spirit of man. He finds it able to multiply and replenish all that its will is set to do. He finds the Spirit of man able to subdue all its world, not by tilling the soil but by knowledge of Good only.

He finds all the corn and gold created before their shadows or earthly symbols are seen. In the realm of man's Spirit they are not sordid, not scanty nor unreliable, but are good throughout. The good corn never fails. The good gold is never scant. They have knowledge in themselves of how to move into the right places and they have a speech with which to speak to the right people. Their substance is Wisdom. To tell this to the world is to set the fine waves of a new era to flowing through the mind of man.

His spirit is within him and its breath is almighty. As he understands it, he is using his mind to step nearer and nearer to his undying Spirit or Mind that he had in the beginning with the God Mind. When once he touches that Mind, all his ideas of matter, evil, people, events are changed into the Original Mind. He sees, hears, smells, tastes, feels as he did at first.

Ezra, the priest (or Esdras, which is the Greek form of the name and when seen must be known as Ezra), thus touched the unvarnished tops of his own God Mind and forgot matter in Spirit, then saw matter and Adam as shadows flung from the God Mind, as that a man might know what power his own mind had and then imagine what it would be not to have power. By him we see that all the operations through which man now moves himself are his God Mind thinking what it would be not to have power, not to be almighty God.

It is God condescending to be man, condescending to be matter, in a thought, which thought, comprehending the whole of creation as we term it, will remember the God Mind from whence it originated and touch by touch on the harp strings of recollection, will finally touch home again. This thought, comprehending all that is called earthly experience, has taken no time to be thought, though it has put in, as a factor of imagining what it would be to be not powerful, that other ingredient of helpless ignorance, what it would be to be subject to time and change.

"Remember now thy Creator in the days of thy youth." Oh, remember and remember till your mind touches the home point before you have put more time into your imagination! Paul says, "If they had only been mindful of the country from whence they came out." All his own practicing was his trying to be mindful. All the original music, all the brilliant touches of mathematics, or the announcement of mighty truths, are men's recollections step by step backward toward their original knowledge. All the meditations of the adepts of India are their endeavor to recollect.

All the struggle of the thinkers of America are the endeavors of mind to step backward to its home point. The home point is in man. There is nowhere he can go that he is not in his home. The home Mind is an eternal, absolute point as unkillable as God, because it is of God. And all that he experiences as man is his thought of what it would be, not to be God.

When he has had enough of such an idea, he may drop it, and what is true may be to him as it was in the beginning, is now, and ever shall be. And what is not true will have no place, as it has none now.

Who has imagined sin, let him know its nature. Who has imagined poverty, let him know its nature. Man is God. Every man is God. What he has chosen to think was his privilege, his power, his ability. When he chose to imagine matter, he had the right. He had the right even to imagine what it would be to be dust. He had the right to be an idea the whole realm of nature. He had the right to call himself Christ or Adam. He had the right to cease to call himself by any other name than his own name and recollect his majesty and bliss as God. He who learns the art of remembering will be called a discoverer.

Genius in its splendor is only attention undistracted to one subject till one realization of something unusual is felt, then another realization, then another. He who has learned how to put his mind upon one thing till that thing has revealed the hidden beauty in one new good after another is practicing memory.

Discovery of Music beyond Beethoven's music will be only the rest of the returning mind on its way of recollecting its God estate.

All the Hindu sacred books were touches of memory. Read their history and see how many of their authors realized that they were not authors but memorizers and how, in order to learn to remember their own Godhood, each mystic learned to remember every statement of God he could gather. He who mixes his imaginations of what it is to be poor, old, sick, feeble, with his statements of God, is like a musician who thinks he must cover himself with pitch and feathers while he is composing. The pitch and feathers distract the attention of his hearers. They take up his own time. They are not necessary. Neither is poverty or pain essential to the religionist's statements of God, but he has distracted himself for ages by making them essential.

God is the undecomposible element, the unmixed principle, the Absolute Knower, whose unchangeable abode is the starting point of man, woman, child, beast, planet, plant, pebble alike.

It is each one's business to recollect for himself. The pebble can remember as well as Esdras. When you find a piece of gold, it is the gold remembering its first estate and touching you on its home journey. When the bags of gold burst open in Washington, it is the first spring of their nature to step out among men in rightful distribution, so realizing one step nearer home.

The stars hear the songs of the men who are now reminding them that all is God. They are gathering up the dropped chords of their ages of time. The sands shine and smile while we repeat the story of the home from whence we came out to imagine what it would be not to be God. They are letting fall their coverings of thought and exposing their glistening hearts. The men of our planet are feeling the springs of the Spirit as we remind ourselves of who we were in the beginning; who we are now, and who we shall be forever. I came forth from God. I know what is not God and what is God. I know now that I am God, and knowing this again, leaving all else, I am in my right Mind.

LESSON X

When mind touches the Absolute it becomes a radiant thing, and men coming in its presence are aware of something out of the ordinary having taken place.

Swedenborg's face shone so after his midnight communings with the Absolute Mind that his servants were frightened. Great miracle workers have overpowered men and women with a nameless power streaming from their presence. They do so in some measure to this day, but as this power seems to leave them when they converse much with men and women or handle material things often, it must be that they approach the Absolute in their praying, for they are not really in touch with it.

All human mind is instrumental. It is not alive. It is not Substance. When it touches the Divine Mind, it is not; this is death. Divine Mind appears; this is Life. As the human mind turns its thoughts and speech upon the Divine Mind, we see a strange shining, we feel a strange power.

Armies always march to victory whose generals touch the Absolute and Eternal Presence while their soldiers sleep.

Mothers who are turning toward the Changeless and Absolute while the waters rage, send ships safely across the stormy waters. Thus it is promised that whatsoever once lays itself on the One Rock of fire nigh the touch of the thoughts, nigh the touch of the fingers shall from thenceforth be undefeatable.

Moses spent thirty years in the mountains turning his thoughts entirely upon the everlasting, unquenchable God. His power was then so great that when he lifted his hands for Pharaoh's army to stand back, it came not upon the Israelites. The Red Sea rolled back. The Israelites walked safely over. Moses called that Eternal One "The Lord." The Absolute Good works and none shall hinder. "Stand ye still and see the salvation. The Lord will fight for you this day."

By whatsoever process you turn the attention of your mind to the Very Present God, it signifies not; you shall touch God by your mind's sight and strike eternal fire for your reward.

There is a practice of breathing seven times deep hoping to touch the Eternal One at the point where the breath leaves off. Many a face glows because the attention has thus been long held toward the Glorious Central God. Many a tongue has startled by its mighty eloquence because the breaths have rolled themselves backward toward the fire point where the Awful Spirit lives and dies not. There, down in the deep bowels shines the fire point. There, back where the minds began, glows the fire point. There, where the breaths extend themselves, blazes the powerful Spirit. So, breathing will lead your mind to the God Mind. Therefore, breathe, ye people, breathe yourselves to death that God may live in you and through you and by you and for you.

"If I make my bed (of attention) in hell, Thou art there. If I ascend up into heaven, Thou art there." [Psalm 139:8] It is to be born of God that the human mind travails.

"Greater love hath no man than this, that a man lay down his life for his friend." Lay down attentions earthward by breathing till you die, that your only Friend, the Lord Jehovah, in whom is everlasting Strength, may live in your place. There is a practice of finding the strings of light that stretch through the airs by giving over, touching and testing all things eternal, that the strings that bind the atoms together may harmonize and vibrate with our attention till touch and taste are dead that the strings divine may live and be our visible life. This is the Soul string like a harp anew and the face glistens like the transfigured man on Mt. Hermon.

"I drew them with the bands of love and they knew not that I healed them."

Touch the strings of light with your attention toward them till you are dead, that they may live in your place. For they are the radiant beams that shine straight from the Absolute God. Laying your whole being on their strong pinions, you are borne to your shining heaven. You are one with God. "The Father and I are One."

There is nothing the wandering attentions of mind are struggling after but to see the Absolute. "The Son can do nothing, only what He seeth the Father do."

The struggling of the instrument is to be alive through death. It longs for the Absolute and Eternal One. It would see that which it cannot and live. None may look upon the Absolute and live. At one supreme moment, taught the Hindus of old, by any process, all acts are abandoned and the heart takes sanctuary with the Absolute. One is that One and nothing less than that One.

"Abandoning all acts, take sanctuary with Me alone. I shall liberate thee from all sins, do thou not grieve."

If a man try the practice of putting his thoughts to one theme alone, there shall come a supreme moment when he understands that one theme. He is It. Then must the theme die in It. That which is Holy Fire in the theme to which a mind has set itself shall live. That which is Holy Fire has burned the rest away. That mind that sets itself to some divine word with some divine meaning must be burned by the meaning of the word till only that which is undying, indestructible Substance is left.

The word God will thus operate. The name Jesus Christ will thus operate. The words "I am I" will thus operate.

At one moment, the uttermost power of the word is reached. All is dead but it. Thus even the brooks are running to death that only the undying and changeless water of life may be visible. The dry sands disappear that only the Spirit may be visible. The fires are burning to death that the deathless fires of One may be seen. The mind of man hastes that it may die for the Absolute Mind to be left. He to whom all the actions of nature are the visible hastening of all things into dissolvable walls is aware that himself is something at his central point that is undissolvable. He sees that all things have also their undissolvable center point. The undying spirit of the water brook, the undying substance of the fire, the deathless center of the wind are all one center.

This knowledge fixes the attention of Mind on Mind, the individual on the undividable. (The individual is the undividable.) Mind is thereby aware that there is one alone—that itself is that One.

As one shakes himself on awakening from slumber, so Mind arouses itself, and its electric fires illuminate Omnipresence. There is nothing but the God Mind. Wherever you look, it is God Center that attracts you. Knowing these two truths, viz., that each center is the God that attracts you, and that it is your own God center that is attracted—you know all that is to be known.

That which seems to be matter is gone by this knowledge. That which seems to be evil is gone by this knowledge. That which seems to be ignorance is gone by this knowledge. That which has been written of knowledge comes thus to pass. "Ye shall know the truth and the truth shall make you free."

The only truth to know of matter is that it is not, for Spirit is all. "I choose to know Spirit rather than to imagine matter," said Spinoza. The whole realm of matter is supposition. Suppose your house should burn? What would you do?

Suppose you were Spirit, free and wise, and should for one instant imagine yourself bound in matter? What would you do? Suppose you, as-free Spirit, were to forget your own free nature? Suppose you saw all the realm of God as bound in flesh? Suppose you saw all the free Spirit of the universe as a mass of ignorance needing instructions, would all your supposings make the facts of the case any different? The choice to know or to suppose is mine and yours. Covering myself with suppositions, I experience earthly conditions. Uncovering my original knowledge, I shine over and transform all things.

At my undefeatable point, I am the Absolute. When I spend the night watches attending to the undefeatable Absolute in the universe, I am laying aside suppositions. I am showing myself. It is no wonder that miracles are wrought by those who know how, by any process whatsoever, to lay off suppositions and strike back upon knowledge.

LESSON XI

If one is born blind or made blind by accident, he educates his fingers to be eyes for him. If one is born deaf, he educates his skin and muscles, his bones and nerves to be ears.

The brain is said to hold in its convolutions a gentle gray matter, a slight agitation of which causes to spring forth the speech and actions of a man. If a large brain has small quantum of gray matter, the man is not intelligent. If a small brain has large store of gray matter, the man is wise. If the fingers and toes of blind people are investigated, it is observed that the brain has transferred some of its gray matter to them, that intelligence may be active through them. The brain by this generous giving declares to all mankind that intelligence dwells not in the brain only, nor is dependent upon brain, but is shed and spread abroad wheresoever it lists to generate gray matter.

Plainly then, gray matter itself is subservient to intelligence and is generated (or not generated) according to intelligence. It cannot distribute or renew itself. Thus, intelligence is master and ruler of the fine etheric substance which acts as intelligence but is naught but an instrument.

It is a great marvel that men have concerned themselves so much with the instruments they use, and so little with the maker of these instruments; for it is clearly to be seen that the maker of an instrument must know how to multiply and replenish it many times over, and if a man could get into the good graces of the Intelligence that forms and manages gray matter, he might get the favor of the marvelous storage thereof and bring forward to the attention of his race, some undreamed-of powers, inventions, helps.

It is evident that the gray matter is but an instrument in some mysterious being's hands. While the scholars in our schools have intensely concerned themselves with this instrument, its maker has been little or not at all regarded. The Hindus have taught for thousands of years that there is a luminous spot in the brain which, being watched steadfastly by the mental eyes, will give one the power to see divine beings. They have taught that as the physical body is warmed, invigorated, strengthened by the sun, so this luminous governor of the head and body is renewed and strengthened by some mighty Spiritual Sun unseen by the eyes of man, unheard by his ears, untouched by his fingers. Only the luminous spot in the brain can see the Spiritual Sun, can feel its warmth, can move in its smile. This luminous spot is the maker of the gray matter. If the luminous governor thereof receives but little light from the Spiritual Sun, it casts but little shade of itself in gray matter, and gray matter being absent, there is then but little man, but little character, but little worth.

The maker of a shadow is the substance that casts it. The substance may stand right in the midst of the shadow. When the sunshine is great enough, the shadow is gone; then the substance is alone in the light. If the luminous spot in the brain is the substance that casts the shade men call gray matter, when it is all shone upon from every direction by the Spiritual Sun, then there cannot be any more gray matter, there cannot be any more flesh man, great or small character, worthy or unworthy will, or sense.

The luminous substance is then all Spiritual Sun. The Spiritual Sun is all there is. As the shadow disappears when it looks toward it, so flesh man with his senses disappears when he looks toward gray matter, his governor. So gray matter disappears when it looks toward the luminous spot, its governor; so the luminous spot disappears when it looks toward the Spiritual Sun, its governor; so the Spiritual Sun disappears when it looks toward the Supreme unnamed Origin of all, the One Starting Point of all that moves or stands still.

If the flesh is under the governorship of gray matter and gray matter under the governorship of the luminous spot, and the luminous spot is under the governorship of the Spiritual Sun, and the Spiritual Sun is under the governorship of the unnamed Origin, the Starting Point of all, it is the business of man's whole being to look utterly away toward the Starting Point of all that is. That Starting Point is the Substance that casts the shadows which we give so many names to. Its only name is the One undescribed Mind. All other mind is but supposition. It is plain that all other mind but It is supposition; for everything that all other mind tells its body or its senses to do is an experiment with both itself and its agent.

Does the musician positively know that his fingers will perform with him at the concert hall tonight? Does he positively know his head will keep level and not get rattled? Does the forensic orator positively know that his thoughts will charm and chain and magnetize his audience this night? Not even the most brilliant mathematician is positive he will not blunder. All is supposition, and vanishes from the memory of the most enrapt listener and observer, so that not an item thereof will remain after a certain lapse of days.

There is a new tide of thought springing forth from man's late discovery that the suppositional life is not worth living. "What is the life that is worth while?" cries man.

Listen: "I am, and there is none beside me." This is the word that streams from the One at the Starting Point.

"Nature is the picture of your thoughts which Thou hast suppressed. Thou hast not known Me. Thou hast supposed something not Me.

"Nature has no actuality. Thou art Nature's painter. On the plastic clouds of nothing nature Thou hast laid your suppositions, and behold trees and rocks and stars. What an artist you can be! Your picture shall all be resolved back into nothingness when you look toward Me.

"When you speak well of My Goodness and majesty, Thou art Jesus Christ."

"When you no longer speak well of My majesty and goodness, but see Me as I am, Thou hast a Science higher than the word. Jesus Christ is the word of majesty and goodness. Jesus Christ gives up the keys of the word of good and truth when He no longer has to speak truth. He is free from the word."

The giving up of even the noblest figures impressed on the walls of existence is Jesus Christ giving up His words. The Jesus Christ Mind sees goodness, majesty, loveliness. Then when goodness, majesty, loveliness have wrought their highest mission, they also cease and that which is independent of all states appears.

The air around men is filled with divine aroma. This is the eternal splendor which he who knows how to find lose[s] himself as he finds it. He breathes the breath thereof and becomes the living Man, Soul, God. He becomes the aroma. It is the all-present, all-pervading Wisdom. It is the breath which the ancients knew would make man God if he breathed, the One Wonderful Presence of whom all things else are shadows. The One Intelligence of whom all other intelligences are suppositions—the One Word, the One Name, that fills the universe, of whom all names are symbols.

The Science of the word as Jesus Christ is the Science of Good and Truth, but the Science that Jesus Christ knows as He gives up the Science of Good and Truth is the Science of the Unspoken Word, the One Name that fills the universe, of whom even Good and Truth are but symbols.

This is the One Substance, the One Intelligence that governs all things. It is the Eternal Refuge, the Everlasting God, The Absolute Wisdom, the glorious Intelligence everywhere One.

Whatsoever is not This is not at all.

LESSON XII

The two ideas "Use" and "Theory" have their adherents among mankind. These adherents despise each other for their idea, not despising their Soul per se.

When we are beloved, we are beloved for our ideas consciously or unconsciously held. When we are disliked, we are disliked for our ideas consciously or unconsciously held. This plane of loving and not loving is the plane of ideas and their demonstrations.

Usefulness is demonstration. An idea not yet worked out into practice is theory. When it is worked out into blood and bones it is usefulness.

The adherents of blood and bones twit the adherents of theories with not living the life. The adherents of theories twit the adherents of bones and blood with living the life too much in the material.

A man may say that a statement is not worth anything till it is made into good eyes and oatmeal. A man may say that a statement is adorable truth whether it has cured your eyes or not; whether it has furnished Coxey's army with oatmeal or not. These men both rejoice when a $100 bill arrives in their hands as the usefulness of their theories. They would not say a word about anything without such self-conviction that they would be satisfied in what they are unclothed of (greenbacks and ideas) if they were utterly free.

The Indian tomahawks his neighbor Indian to get his wampum. The Yankee tomahawks his neighbor Yankee to get his greenbacks. The Religionist tomahawks his neighbor religionist to get his ideas. The only difference between the Religionist and the Indian is that the Indian will hug and kiss and love the captured wampum, while the Religionist will strike and crush the captured idea.

Whoever standing calmly and coolly by the battle of uses and theories and touches them not, but utterly detached from either money, wampum, religious principle or men who wrangle, knows them for what they are and knows himself as free from either, knows himself as he is—he only is secure.

Security is the aim of the adherents of theories. Security is the aim of the adherents of uses. Security means out of reach of vanquishment, out of reach of necessity, out of reach of contention, out of reach of effort.

The doctrine of Jesus Christ is entirely of security. The "secure man" was His theme. His Name is God-man. He is the Father and the Father is He. That is, He is that secure First Mind that is not entangled with wampum, oatmeal, money, or religious ideas. The Brahmin religions said He is the unattached One, but the Secure One will not be reached by tomahawking bodies or tomahawking religions. Ages of tomahawks have proved this proclamation.

The Secure One is that one who is reached by leaving principle of adherence and being no adherent. All the adhering tendency being dropped, I am unburdened sufficiently to turn about and face my Secure Self. That Secure Self is the One that the prophets, the priests, the millionaires, the Czars, the mayors, the operators are squabbling to be.

Oh, Thou, Mighty One! I see that Thou art not reached by effort. Thou art reached by facing Thee, released from efforts.

Thou needest not to toil and moil. You need not to use wampum. Thou needest not to use money. Thou needest not to use religion. Thou needest not to be praised. Thou needest not to be watching out for the main chances to cut thy way through squabbling money grabbers or squabbling religionists. Thou needest not to make thy living. Thou hast no debts to pay. Thou hast no position to hold. Thou hast nothing to hold. Thou needest nothing.

Wonderful One! How easy it is to envy Thee. This is the envy that reaches security. Thy unweighted, unattached indifference—I, by envying, become secure.

Thou art the One of whom I am jealous, for Thou sittest on that throne I have been squabbling with ideas and hands to secure. This is the jealousy that reaches security, for it keeps me watching Thee; and watching Thee, I secure Thee. I am Thee.

If Thou hast that security from struggle, that security from fear, that security from danger, that security from money, that security from religion, that the Czars and the ministers are hating each other in order to capture, how can I help hating Thee. This is the malice which reaches security, for it keeps me watching Thee. Anything that keeps me watching Thee is a freeing from adherences. It is a sight of security to watch Thee, though I watch Thee by fighting Thee, for it makes me forget wampum and money and people and religion. I remember only Thee.

I see Thee while I fight Thee, and I remember this is Jesus Christ taking the Kingdom by force. "The Kingdom of Heaven suffereth violence and the violent take it by force."

I, like Jacob, fight Thee for Thy security. Give it to me. "I will not let Thee go except Thou bless me." If I have contention, it shall be with Thee. What is squabbling man that should contend with him for that which he has not? Thou hast what I have panted after since time was.

To look toward Thee is to secure Thy security. Hast Thou not always spoken, "Turn unto Me"? See! I wrestle with Thee, Thou Secure One. I am after all that Thou art and have. I will not let Thee go except Thou give me Thyself.